Story Weaving

Using Stories to Transform Your Congregation

Peter M. Morgan

CBP Press
St. Louis, Missouri

Unless otherwise indicated, all scripture quotations are from the Revised Standard Version of the Bible, copyrighted 1946, 1952, © 1971, 1973, by the Division of Christian Education of the National Council of the Churches of Christ in the United States of America, and used by permission. Quotations identified as KJV are taken from the King James Version of the Bible.

Library of Congress Cataloging-in-Publication Data

Morgan, Peter M.
  Story weaving.

  1. Storytelling—Religious aspects—Christianity.   2. Christian fiction.
  I. Title.
BT78.M83   1986   251   86-6079
ISBN 0-8272-3423-6

Contents

Acknowledgments

An essential feature of renewal is the weaving together of persons in supportive enterprise. Writing this book was an experience in renewal. My work has been woven with the supportive enterprise of many friends.

Primarily, I acknowledge De Vee, John, Lyle, Marjorie, and all the other friends in the church whose stories, woven into my own, make the gospel come alive. I dedicate this work to them with gratitude.

Others have supported the specific work of preparing the manuscript. Lynne, my wife, kindly and quietly made my imaginative spelling and punctuation publicly presentable. Joyce Coalson, Harold Johnson, Ann Updegraff-Spleth, colleagues in the Division of Homeland Ministries, have been generous in time and attention given to refining my thoughts and expressing them clearly. Ronald Allen of Christian Theological Seminary and Linda Chenoweth of St. Louis made valuable comments on the chapters on preaching and worship. Raymonda Unger conscientiously typed the manuscript.

I am indebted to the sponsors of three lectureships who gave me the opportunity to develop my ideas on congregational revitalization: The Ministers' Workshop and Oreon E. Scott Lectures of Bethany College, West Virginia, 1983; the Mary Edgerton Memorial Lectures of First Christian Church, Aurora, Nebraska, 1984; The Colleges of The Church of Christ of Canada Lectureship, given at the Disciples' Maritimes Assembly, 1985.

I have experienced personal renewal through the support of these friends. It is my hope that my friends and I will be welcomed in the supportive enterprise of helping the readers lead their congregations to new vitality.

Introduction

Story Weaving is a "how to" book in that it presents a method that may contribute to congregational vitality. That method will be presented in the context of a discussion of congregational renewal. The method responds to the hunger of mainline Christians for authentic religious experiences in their churches.

Generally, I hold "how to . . ." books in some disdain. No matter what is printed on the cover of the book, when my eyes see "How to . . .," my mind finishes the phrase ". . . Become Handsome, Pretty, Sexy, Wealthy, and Powerful by Being Earnest, Diligent, and/ or Obnoxious."

"How to" books overpromise. That would have been the case with a book titled "How to Revitalize Your Mainline Congregation." How can anyone seriously suggest that all of the complexity of factors in millions of unique persons in thousands of unique congregations be controlled by the information in one book? A more accurate title is, "A Consideration of the Methodology of Storytelling as a Means of Evoking Religious Experiences That May Enhance the Vitality of Mainline Congregations." That title would be more suitable for an eighteenth-century tract. So we're back to "How to Become Handsome, Pretty, Sexy. . . ." I almost did it again. The title is *Story Weaving: Using Stories to Transform Your Congregation.*

In addition to some "how-to" material, the book is a collection of stories. Please help yourself to them. This margin mark and Appendix A will help you find them. Enjoy reading them. Enjoy reshaping them in your own style. Enjoy retelling them. Enjoy the other stories they call to mind. Enjoy the stories prompted in others who hear these stories.

Enjoy the revitalizing moments that come as grace gifts when you see yourself no longer alone but woven into a community of God's storytellers of yesterday, today, and tomorrow.

Epiphany, 1986   Peter M. Morgan

Chapter 1

Spinning Yarns

Stories can transform lives.

Chuck and Edna reminisced, "Remember when Debbie was born. . . ." "Remember when David was the neighborhood grass cutter. . . ." From each memory spun a story and a smile. They saved one of the best yarns for last. "Remember when we went to California in 1957. . . ." The story spun off memories of saving the money, planning the route, and the adventures on the way from Iowa to California and home again.

The stories we choose to remember and retell have power. They are the lens through which we understand life. They teach us values. They guide our decisions. We choose to tell certain stories and omit others because some are magnets that draw meanings from many experiences. They contain more than just the incident recited. They portray our values and re-energize our commitment to a particular life view.

Chuck and Edna's trip to California was a venture that the family was capable of facing together and enjoying. The trip was important. Just as important, however, has been retelling the story of the trip. The story affirms Chuck and Edna's belief that their life is a venture that they are capable of facing and enjoying. That belief is fostered and nourished because of such stories as the California trip. Because they tell those stories, life is for them, in fact, a venture to be enjoyed together. Stories have power.

Stories can also transform lives in unfortunate ways. Joan and Terry, like Chuck and Edna, also play "Remember when. . . ." Sadly, the tale they frequently choose to retell is of a mother-in-law's ill-advised remark about her future son-in-law during Joan and Terry's courtship. That story, too, has become a magnet around which is clustered feelings of resentment and family rejection. The retelling of that story contributes to a deteriorating marriage. Stories have power!

Stories can transform congregations.

You may well have experienced this every-Sunday incident. You go into worship determined to catch every word, meaning, and nuance of the sermon. The service goes along satisfactorily— an opening of music and prayer, the service of the Word in which the scripture lessons are well read. Now comes the sermon and you bring all your senses to full attention. Eight minutes later the preacher is wading through a muddy bog of abstractions and generalizations. You realize your eyes are glazed over, invisible plugs cover your ears. Despite your best intentions, you haven't caught every word, meaning, and nuance. Then something almost magical happens! The preacher simply says, "Let me tell you what happened last Wednesday. . . ." Your eyes clear, your ears open, your brain becomes receptive, you sit up, you slide to the front of the pew. You don't even know if it is going to be an interesting story; you just know a story is coming. Stories can bring the church to alertness, attentiveness. They bring new energy. Stories are potentially powerful enough to transform mainline congregations, even *your* mainline congregation.

This book is for persons in mainline congregations. Our congregations are part of the older denominations of North America. They wear "brand name" labels: Brethren, Episcopal, Disciples, Lutheran, Methodist, Presbyterian, and United Church of Christ.

Many of us are concerned because we have experienced a decline in our congregations. They are fewer and they are smaller. Sometimes morale gets low. My own church, the Christian Church (Disciples of Christ), had 1,503,004 members in 5,186 congregations in 1960 when I became pastor of a student congregation. In 1985, we were 1,121,301 souls in 4,214 congregations.

At the same time, we have seen the "edge of town" congregations move "uptown." Little handfuls of people with conservative theology and enthusiastic worship have now become large congregations with prosperous budgets and impressive buildings. They have moved toward public acceptance and authentication in the centers of power. These congregations of the younger American denominations have become politically influential. Formerly, mayors were thought of as "Presbyterian types." Now mayors' offices are more frequently occupied by persons with images suitable to the "moral majority."

By comparison to the fervent activity and growth of these congregations, our older, mainline congregations appear to just plod along. Sometimes they don't even plod along anymore.

Many of us know the pain of loss. Congregations die. Families who have been members of our congregations for generations become discouraged and disenchanted. They become divorced from the old family church. Some drop out. Some are attracted to the newer, energetic, conservative congregations and change their memberships. We are painfully aware of our lack of vitality. If not, someone like Heather will remind us.

Heather's Circus Report

The truth in the story of Heather's circus report makes us laugh and cry at the same time. Eight-year-old Heather, still wide-eyed with the excitement of seeing her first circus, came stumbling into the den bursting to tell her mother of her adventure. She went on and on about the funny clowns, the beautiful ladies flying through the air, the big elephants. She concluded her tale by declaring, "O Mama, it was so exciting that if you ever went to the circus you would never be satisfied with going to church again!"

The purpose of this work is to bring together the need for renewal of the mainline congregations and the power of stories to be renewing. You, the reader, I imagine to be active in a mainline congregation. You probably have been or are now or soon will be a leader in the church: pastor, moderator, elder, committee head, seminary student, deacon, nominee for office. As we go together through the pages of this book, we will discover the sources for stories that can renew our congregations: the Bible, persons near to us, persons who have gone before us, persons in the worldwide church. We will look for patterns in what has been happening to our churches. Does history give us clues? What insight does Scripture give us into God's gift of renewal to the faithful? We will move then to some very specific applications. Suggestions will be offered for using "story weaving" in our congregations.

This book is not just about stories. It is also a book of stories. Stories will be told. I will share some of the stories that have renewed my own life and ministry. I have told these stories across

9

North America in sermons, lectures, and workshops. Many who heard them report the stories have helped renew their own ministries. More importantly, the stories have awakened their own stories. That is how I suggest you read the book. Read it actively. Dialogue with the concepts of renewal. From my stories discover your own stories! Write yourself notes on ways to begin "story weaving" activities in your congregation.

Where I grew up in southern West Virginia, telling stories was called spinning yarns. If we are to have stories to weave, we will need some yarn. How do stories work? Where do our stories come from? How do we work with stories?

How do stories work? They engage us. They invite participation. They evoke response. In the telling and hearing of stories, experiences are created and shared. Rather than a story being an illustration to help people understand a concept, the story itself is the point. Stories are not to answer the question, "Do you get it?" Rather they ask the question, "What do you think of that?" They invite, "Let's talk about our experiences, thoughts, feelings."

Stories become entry points into the spiritual realm of a person's life. Religion is more than an idea. It engages what Jonathan Edwards called the "affections."

> Take away all love and hatred, all hope and fear, all anger, zeal, and affectionate desire, and the world would be in a great measure motionless and dead; there would be no such thing as activity amongst mankind, or any earnest pursuit whatsoever. . . . And as in worldly things worldly affections are very much the spring of men's motion and action; so in religious matters the spring of their actions is very much religious affection: he that has doctrinal knowledge and speculation only, without affection, never is engaged in the business of religion.[1]

The "affective level" is where our lives are transformed. The affective level is where we may become transformed and thereafter transform our congregations. The entryway to the affections is often through stories. The language that communicates with the affections is story.

John Westerhoff in *A Pilgrim People* shares his insights on the nature of stories.

> Stories are concrete and particular. They are not expressions of doctrine or universal truth. Stories are open-ended. They are not to be read literally; as a matter of fact, stories give the storyteller freedom in their retelling. Stories stimulate the imagination. There is

not only one interpretation of a story; indeed, the listener is encouraged to listen freely and discover personal meaning. . . . Stories are the bottom line of human communal life: Nothing else is ultimately needed.[2]

Where do our stories come from? Stories inspire stories. A few years ago hundreds of thousands of Americans were enthralled by the stories of a veterinarian as told under the name of James Herriot. One day I sat enjoying *All Creatures Great and Small*. I felt myself getting caught up in the stories. I kept trying to remain detached. "It's only a story. It's only a story," I kept repeating. But I was captivated. I read on and despite myself a tear would come to the corner of my eye as a story turned sad. My knuckles would turn white with anger at a story of cruelty. I laughed at the pranks.

Later I reflected on the power of the stories. They had power over me even when I decided they would not. Even when I kept repeating, "It's only a story," I laughed, my knuckles turned white, I shed a tear. I was struck by the power of stories.

I then said to myself that my life as a pastor is at least as fascinating as that of a veterinarian in rural England. I and the people in the congregation experience powerful, fascinating, moving, funny stories almost every day if we have ears and eyes to hear and see them. I then began to discover life in the church as the adventure it is. I began to have eyes and ears to see and hear the stories of the Bible, church tradition, the global church, the ecumenical movement, persons near me and my own autobiography. I then began to "spin the yarns."

THE BIBLE

In weaving, the loom is set up with yarn of the warp in place. The yarn of woof shuttles back and forth and is woven into the warp. The Bible is the warp of the church's story weaving. John Westerhoff defines the Bible as a storybook.

". . . it is a love story between God and humanity; it is a story of a covenant made, broken, and renewed, again and again. God as creator, redeemer, and perfecter loves each creature, personally and as members of the whole human community. In return, we are expected to love God ourself, and each other."[3]

The church is a story-formed community. God uses stories to call us together, to give us identity, to focus our energies on

11

mission and purpose, and to guide how we relate to each other, to persons and groups outside our fellowship, to nature, to history, and to the arts.

Once Upon a Time

Imagine yourself seated with our biblical ancestors around a desert campfire. As the children huddle near the fire and we adults blanket them against the desert night chill, they ask questions of "How come . . .!" "How come we wander the desert and others are settled in towns?" "How come there are earth and sky?" "How come some people tend sheep while others grow crops; some people work as blacksmiths and others as tentmakers and some do other work?"

The old ones of the circle began to answer the little ones' "how comes." "Once upon a time there was a beautiful garden called paradise. . . ." The stories have begun that continue through the night and on through the centuries. Those stories call us together and keep us together.

We can go on through the pages of the Bible to read and hear the stories that formed us. The Exodus from slavery. At the seder meal in the homes of our Jewish friends, a child asks the head of the house, "Why is this day different from all other days?" The "once upon a time" of the Exodus is retold. In Scripture those "once upon a times," which are the basis of all of our stories, continue to spin out and to weave us into the fabric of the people of God. The story of a judge named Deborah; the story of a reluctant preacher named Jonah; the story of the young widow Ruth; the story of the prophet who wept, Jeremiah; the story of. . . .

Once Upon a Time, Continued

Then once upon a time there was a boy-child cradled in a manger because the inn was oversold. That boy-child became a man and a storyteller. "Once upon a time a man was going down from Jerusalem to Jericho. . . ." "Once upon a time there was a widow with two pennies. . . ." The stories go on and on about that storyteller Jesus and those of us drawn to him and his stories.

Once upon a time some of Jesus' followers got into trouble because they healed a lame man (Acts 3—4). Once upon a time some suffering Gentile converts received a letter from the leader of the Jewish Christians (1 Peter). Those stories spun on through the centuries until once upon a time a parent, teacher, friend, pastor, spouse, or child told you the great stories of God's "once upon a time." You too were then woven into the story-formed community of the people of God.

Stories of the Bible are the warp through which we weave the stories of our lives. Stories of the Bible are basic to the life *and* revitalized life of the congregation. Stories enliven all that the church does. We can understand preaching as weaving personal stories into the biblical stories in such a way that lives are transformed. Preaching is important. We can understand evangelism as helping persons outside the faith weave their stories into God's story in such a way that they freely respond in faith and participation in the church. Outreach is important. We can understand vital participation in the church as weaving our stories and the stories of people of faith with the biblical stories in such a way as to empower God's mission for the church. Christian community is important. The biblical story is basic.

One of the major tasks of the mainline congregation is helping its people know the biblical stories. We need to help people know those stories as the beginning of the ongoing love story between God and us, his people. The Bible's stories are told as the story of our people. It is our story.

Not Them, But Us

Michael ben Avi showed me the sights of his country, Israel. We walked over the archaeological sites. He told the stories of the people who had inhabited those places. He didn't tell the story of "those people" or "them." He told how "we" built the wall, "we" came to the altar. The biblical story is our story to know and love and retell. It is the basis for renewal.

God's story is to weave into our stories. A couple walked on a road toward a village called Emmaus. They discussed the troubling events of the last few days. A feast in the city, an execution, reports of a resurrection. A stranger came to walk beside them. In the conversation he wove the story they told into the story of Scripture. After the weaving of the stories the couple later broke bread with the stranger. He was a stranger no more. They knew him to be the living Christ. They reflected on their story, "Did not our hearts burn within us while he talked to us on the road, while he opened to us the scriptures?" (Luke 24:32).

Story weaving has been going on throughout the history of our people. The New Testament weaves the Scripture of its people, our Old Testament, throughout its narrative. The story was not primarily told by formal public rhetoric. One of the words we connect to preaching is homily. That word in Greek is *homileo*, which is in the Emmaus story and translates "talking." "That very day two of them were going to a village named Emmaus . . . and *talking* with each other about all these things that had happened" (Luke 24:13-14). Story weaving is working biblical stories into our own lives through prayerful reflection and conversation.

Where do we get yarn for weaving? The yarn of the warp is from the Bible. In addition to the Bible, the larger fellowship of Christians is also a source of our story-weaving yarn. Here is the advantage of being a mainline church. Tradition, apostolic continuity, global mission and ecumenism, persons near us, our theological autobiography are a great repertoire of stories. Those stories are woof to weave into the warp of the Bible story. We will explore those sources for stories, then we will see how they can transform congregations.

CHURCH TRADITION

We are in the continuity of the apostolic tradition. The stories of and about Jesus and his first followers have been continuously passed from generation to generation. Peter and Andrew and Mary Magdalene told the stories. Those stories were woven into the lives of their children and their neighbors' children. The church, the story-formed community, wove the stories of the apostles into its life and passed the story to the next generation. The actions of weaving the biblical story into each generation and then having them add their own story has given us the rich and varied resource of church tradition. It is a big ball of yarn.

We of the mainline church find much of our strength and authority in Tradition. Tradition is the cumulative experience of God's people under the power and guidance of the Holy Spirit. God's Spirit did not cease to function when the last apostle died or when the last book was selected to be included in the Bible. That Spirit has been evident in the continuity of the biblical story being woven throughout church history. Turn the pages of church history. Glance down at random. Often you will find someone story weaving the biblical story into his or her own story. Those continuing stories are a part of our total story as a church today.

Polycarp and Peter

The well-known stories of story weaving in the Tradition come easily to mind.

In the second century Polycarp, an overseer of the church, Bishop of Smyrna, stood before the emperor's proconsul. The proconsul sought a way to save the old bishop's life. "Have regard for your age. Swear by the genius of Caesar. Swear and I will dismiss you."

Polycarp replied, "Eighty and six years have I served Christ, and He never did me wrong; how can I now blaspheme my King that has saved me?"

Later, as the executioner lit the fire that killed him, Polycarp prayed, "Father of thy well-beloved Son, Jesus Christ, through whom we have received knowledge of thee. . . . I bless thee that thou hast thought me worthy of the present day and hour, to have a share in the number of martyrs, and in the cup of Christ, unto the resurrection. . . . May I be received in thy spirit, this day, as a rich and acceptable sacrifice."

Old Bishop Polycarp had prepared for his martyrdom by spending days in prayer. When we read from Polycarp's writing, we discover one of the prayer resources that must have been with him as he prepared to die. Time and time again he quotes the letter of 1 Peter.

Peter, facing the shadow of his own cross, was moved to write this letter to the Gentile converts who were being persecuted in Asia Minor.

Now across the centuries we look back and listen to Polycarp taking strength for his pending death by looking and listening to Peter giving courage to the Gentiles. Across the centuries we hear the murmur of Polycarp and the saints who have suffered as they prayerfully read the words of Peter.

"He himself [Christ] bore our sins in his body on a tree, that we might die to sin and live to righteousness" (1 Peter 2:24). "Through him you have confidence in God, who raised him from the dead and gave him glory, so that your faith and hope are in God" (1 Peter 1:21).

The continuous weaving of the story of Peter's letter to the suffering Gentiles helps us believe that we do not suffer alone. Christ and the saints of history share our suffering with us; Christ and the saints of history share their glory with us.

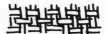 **Martin and Paul**

Stop the pages of your history book in the sixteenth century and find this story of a saint weaving the biblical story into his life. The bright young German professor and monk, Martin Luther, prayed earnestly, fervently for years in front of the stern glare of a vengeful Christ. The mere sight of a crucifix brought back the experience of the night he was struck by lightning. In that moment of panic he had pledged to Saint Anne to become a monk.

For years Luther trembled in prayer before a vengeful Christ. Then one night all was quietly changed. Martin Luther was simply reading Romans when he received the words, ". . . the just shall live by faith" (Romans 1:17, KJV). Luther tells us that at that quiet moment when the biblical word became his word, "I felt myself reborn and to have gone through open doors to paradise."

John and Paul

Let yourself stop along the continuous procession of the faithful for a life-changing moment in the eighteenth century. The biblical story was woven into the life of John Wesley. He describes that life-changing experience.

"In the evening [of May 24, 1738,] I went very unwillingly to a society in Aldersgate Street, where one was reading Luther's *Preface to the Epistle to the Romans*. About a quarter before nine, while he was describing the change which God works in the heart through faith in Christ, I felt my heart strangely warmed."[4]

We look back on a continually unfolding story. We look back to Polycarp as he looked to Peter as he looked to Christ. Our courage and hope are stirred. We look back to Wesley who looked back to Luther as he looked to Paul. Our faith is born anew.

God's Spirit sees to it that the weaving goes on. What precious yarns we have from Scripture and Tradition for doing the work of story weaving. We weave the story of God's continuing revitalization of his people.

The Bible and apostolic tradition are sources of the yarns that renew us. The global community of the church also spins its yarns for our enrichment. We of the mainline churches value inclusiveness. Even for us Protestants Pope John Paul II is our shepherd whose pastoral guidance we may argue against, but must consider seriously. Desmond Tutu is not just an Anglican bishop in South Africa. He represents to us too the unity and apostolic continuity of the church and its courage to seek justice.

THE GLOBAL CHURCH

Knowing persons from the global Christian community and learning their stories are sources of renewal and vitality for mainline congregations of North America. Our miniature tapestry of church becomes larger and more colorful when we discover who we really are as a worldwide, world-loving people. One of the tasks that contribute to renewal of congregations is listening to, learning, retelling, and "weaving" into our stories the stories of our brothers and sisters in Christ from around the world.

In this story sharing we move one step further from the old scheme of paternalistic mission. We take one more step away from dominating younger churches in other lands. Equality and mutual benefit are expressed in the giving and receiving of stories across cultural and national boundaries.

The fabric of who we are is much more interesting when it is woven with threads, yarns, of friends in Christ from Moscow and Cairo and Jakarta and San Juan.

Please, Please Bring Jacinta

David Vargas, my friend and colleague, tells this story from his home in Puerto Rico. Samuel Pagan sat before a doctoral examination committee in a North American school and was asked by one of his learned colleagues, "Who is the theological thinker who most influenced your thinking and your life?"

The answer came quickly, "Jacinta Diaz."

Jacinta Diaz? Jacinta Diaz? Jacinta Diaz? The professors sorted through their memories for the Latin American theologian Jacinta Diaz. Samuel answered their puzzled expressions with a story.

"Jacinta Diaz was a member of my congregation in rural Puerto Rico. She was not an outspoken leader in the church or an officeholder or public figure. She was known, however, as a person of great faith. Even people outside the church in our small town knew her as a faith person. She was thought of as the one in the village whose prayers God would most likely answer.

"Her son was not of the church, but was most deeply loved by his mother. One night he was relaxing in an open country bar a half mile from our town. Angry words flared. Threats turned to fighting. The fighting got out of control. Her son lay dead on the floor of the bar.

"In the small town the word of the tragedy spread quickly. Jacinta and a few friends were together in her home pouring out their anguished grief.

"The bar was in turmoil. The body lay on the floor. The young man who had killed her son was in a crisis of remorse at his impulsive violence. He cried, 'What have I done, what have I done.' He talked of taking his own life. In his despair he cried, 'Please, please bring Jacinta.' He did not even realize that it was Jacinta's son whom he had killed.

18

"Word comes to Jacinta's house of the young man's pleas. A neighbor says, 'This man must be crazy, he wants you to comfort him!' Jacinta rises from her grief, walks from her house, down the half mile of country road, into the bar. There she speaks quietly, she puts healing hands on her son's killer, she prays with him."

Samuel Pagan's "greatest theologian" walks from a dusty road in Puerto Rico to be part of our story. In the awe-filled silence after the story we realize we have much to learn in living our Christian compassion. We also realize we can come closer to full compassion in our lives because we have stood uneasily in the presence of compassion in the story of Jacinta Diaz.

THE ECUMENICAL MOVEMENT

The ecumenical movement gives us access to stories that can become part of the fabric of renewed congregations. The stories of persons and churches of other denominations in our communities can instruct us. In the listening and telling of stories, the *koinonia*, the shared participation in Christ can expand.

World leaders of the church come to us through their writing or speaking to tell stories. They help us see ourselves in mirrors held before us from other Christian people in other places. Michael Crosby shares a story and his reflections on the Eucharist in an ecumenical setting.

Taking Brokenness into Ourselves

"One cannot eat the bread that is broken without accepting responsibility to do something about all the brokenness that is still part of the body. One cannot be recognized or known by God if one does not recognize Christ in his broken members (cf. Luke 24:35).

"This realization struck me forcefully during a liturgy in which I participated while taking a Spanish course. It was at a time when attempts to learn the language had become particularly difficult and burdensome for the class. We met for the breaking of the bread.

"A sister in our group not only was having a hard time being reconciled to a new language but also was suffering from much irreconciliation in the community from which she came. During the shared homily, she revealed her brokenness and weakness to the extent that she left the room in tears.

"When I was handed the bread consecrated as the body of Jesus, the realization came to me that this broken bread in my hand contained her brokenness. This immediately brought me into solidarity with her as well as with other broken people about whom I had particular concern—the Wisconsin farmer I talked to each day who needed rain for his crops, the millions of starving in the Sahel who lacked food itself. I understood there that by saying 'Amen' to consecrated bread, I would become responsible for the healing of all these people, not just her."[5]

Our vision is expanded as we hear a story from another ecumenical leader.

 ### An Unseen Masterpiece

An officer in the National Council of Churches was invited to help lead worship in a service to be televised from Israel. The calendar was cleared. Funding from the television network was arranged. She was off to Israel.

Later, after she had settled into her hotel, she decided to visit the site of the service. It was a very old, small church under the care of a monastic community. The church was a bit run-down. It hadn't been modernized with electrical power.

As she looked around, a fascinating scene played before her. The television crew was busy going about its work of setting up generators, stringing cables, mounting cameras to stands, placing microphones. The monks, hushed and standing back against the walls, were hosts, but in the face of all this activity and modernity, seemed like guests from another century.

Something extraordinary happened as the scene played on. The technicians began to test the lights. The whole dark chapel flamed to light. Some of the monks looked up, nudged their brothers. Soon they were all pointing upward. The monks then vanished. Presently they scurried back bringing the entire community to see what they had seen.

A member of their order, in a forgotten century long ago, had erected a scaffold and had quietly painted by candlelight an unseen masterpiece meant for the eyes of God only.

These old mainline congregations of ours are places of story. From the church of the ages come stories. From the global church come stories. From the ecumenical movement come stories. They help us to notice the little masterpieces meant for the eyes of God only. In those stories we discover the church, and our congregations as an expression of the church, to be a people in the vital venture of weaving God's story into our own story.

PERSONS NEAR US

Stories come from people near us in the pulpits and pews of our local churches. Stories come even from those like us who may have a difficult time being wholly attentive throughout a sermon. As we have ears to hear and eyes to see those stories, we discover the lives of the people near us have moments when they are "quiet little masterpieces."

How do we develop eyes to see and ears to hear those stories? Let me offer one of the devotional exercises that I use to see and hear the stories. The exercise uses story weaving. From meditation on Scripture there plays before me the stories of persons with whom I am now sharing or have shared life. This exercise has six actions. First, a prayer for illumination. We prayerfully approach the Scripture as a word from our beloved. I frequently use this prayer: "O God, prepare the soil of my heart so that your Word may take root, mature, and come into harvest in my life of ministry. Through Jesus Christ, the sower of the seed. Amen." Second, read the passage slowly, looking for people or things about people: characters, the original readers/hearers, advice to those who first heard or read the passage. Give yourself time to slowly reread and focus your concentration on people in the biblical story. Third, bring to mind one or two people you know or knew personally who are suggested by the text. Take time to experience what those people are like for you. Explore why those persons came to mind. Fourth, recall the specific stories told about or by those persons, or the moments you have shared with them. Fifth, write in a journal your paraphrase of the text and one or two of the stories. Sixth, pray for the persons who have come to you in your meditation.

With hesitancy, I invite you into one of my very private moments of story weaving. I share the text and two stories woven into it. The text is Galatians 5:22-25 on the fruit of the Spirit. "But the fruit of the Spirit is love, joy, peace, patience, kindness, goodness, faithfulness, gentleness, self-control; against such there is no law. And those who belong to Christ Jesus have crucified the flesh with its passions and desires. If we live by the Spirit, let us also walk by the Spirit."

After the prayer for illumination I slowly read the text looking for characters. There were none. I then tried to recall the original hearers. I had a vague recollection of Paul writing to the young churches of Galatia, which were being split apart by someone who had come after him. I imagined faces scowling in distrust and alienation. Next, I reread the characteristics of the fruit of the Spirit and asked, "Whom do I know who responds with such grace when they have been in situations of possible distrust, misunderstanding, and alienation?" I immediately thought of Frank.

 **A Monument to Decency**

The proudest time in Frank's life was when he wore the uniform of the U.S. Army and defended this country he loves in World War II.

When Frank came back from the war, he became the town cobbler with his shoe shop right on the town square. Frank and his shoe shop were a monument to decency and fairness just like the statue in the square. About that time Frank and Gertie started their family. He became known in church and town as a Bible-studying, praying Christian.

Twenty years later Frank knew the turmoil and anguish of a son who seemingly defiled everything that Frank valued. Steven did not love what his country was doing in Vietnam. He was repulsed by the sight of a military uniform. Steve's defiance was so strong that he eventually went to jail. What agony for Frank who loved his son and loved his country.

The time came for Steven to be released. What was to happen? If you stopped in at Frank's shoe shop, in the summer of '69, you would see the answer. Frank would put his arm around Steven and say, "I want you to meet my new partner." Some people thinly veiled their disgust. Customers were lost. Others thought of the words ". . . the fruit of the Spirit is love, joy, peace, patience, kindness, goodness, faithfulness, gentleness, self-control."

There is an update on Frank and Steve. Frank is retired now. It's been fifteen years since Steve came home. Steve is in charge now. The shoe shop is still on the square. Now Steven is recognized as a monument to decency and fairness like the statue in the square and his father before him.

In my meditation on persons described by Galatians 5:22-25, I also remembered Pauline.

Courage on Wheels

When I met Pauline, she had already been homebound for almost ten years. She has multiple sclerosis. Most of those ten years had been spent alone. Her husband worked long hours. She had little company except those who came and went to look after her physical needs. One long minute after another—hour after hour, day after day, week after week, year after year—ten years virtually alone.

But Pauline was not a defeated, bitter, small-minded person. She took what little she had and made the most of it. She had a little pile of cards from the early days of her illness—the ones with Helen Steiner Rice poems were her favorites—and she had her Christian radio station. Hardly the things I would recommend to fight the demons of physical incapacitation and loneliness. Yet Pauline took what she had, appreciated it, used it, and was blessed by it. In the solitude of that lonely room Pauline cultivated a relationship with God. Her life showed the fruit of the Spirit: love, joy, peace, patience, kindness, goodness, faithfulness, gentleness, self-control. When people of the church started visiting Pauline, she said, "To experience love like this means something good has come from my disease that I might not have known otherwise."

There is now an update on Pauline. In recent years, she inherited some money. She got herself a van and had it fitted out with a lift for her wheelchair. Pauline gets out now. She not only worships God in the solitude of her room, she gathers to worship God with cherished friends who visited her. On the days Pauline is in church the hymns of praise are a little more vibrant.

In my prayers for Frank and Steve and Pauline, I also prayed my gratitude for knowing them.

OUR THEOLOGICAL AUTOBIOGRAPHY

When we have eyes to see and ears to hear, we discover stories in our own lives. Of course, our own personal stories have the greatest power to transform our lives and to prepare us to be people who contribute to the revitalization of our congregation. Eyes that see and ears that hear our own stories can be cultivated in prayer and meditation. I call it theological autobiography.

 ### The Old Black Preacher

Perspiration glistened off of the preacher's blue/black skin. He stopped for a moment, took out a large handkerchief, and mopped his face. The congregation settled, awaiting his next words.

He quietly told the story of his grandmother picking cotton as a slave in South Carolina. She had sung, "Nobody knows the trouble I'se seen—Nobody knows, but Jesus." The freshly mopped face of the old preacher glistened again, this time with the tears of painful memory of his grandmother's life, his family's life, his own life.

"Nobody knows but Jesus." The old preacher still had fire as he preached on about "Nobody knows but Jesus." The preaching became a part of a moving congregational dance, people swaying, clapping, and shouting.

Often the intensity of life in the present prevents us from seeing and hearing the stories of the ways God is present in our lives. After some time has elapsed, we can engage in prayerful remembering of an episode in our life. Then the eyes see, the ears hear the story of personal good news.

We see more clearly looking at the past than at the present. Some tongue-in-cheek biblical interpretation helps us weave this discovery into the scriptural story. Why are the events of the Exodus reported in contradictory tones? Often the report comes

24

as a tale of adventure. "Isn't it amazing? We were freed from slavery in Egypt and sent on our way to claim a land of promise. God fed us. God guided us with a moving cloud by day, a pillar of fire by night. God sent a powerful man Moses to lead us." Other times the same tale is told in quite different terms. "My feet are tired. Forty years to go two hundred miles. First we go this way, then that way. Can't Moses make up his mind? What a wishy-washy leader. At least in Egypt we had a dependable place to stay and three meals a day. Speaking of food—manna, manna, manna. I sure am tired of manna. We've been wandering all these years. We're tired. Now they expect us to kill giants to get the land that was promised." Why is the story told from such contradictory points of view? We can imagine the tellers of the complaining version had tired feet, were tired of manna, and were afraid of the Canaanites. The tellers of the tale of adventure were secure in their homes looking back to relive a great moment. A more serious understanding of the story's interpretation is that it reports the reality of the Exodus, including the tired feet. Yet, after time passed, the story was told, tired feet included, as an event when God was powerfully near.

God is powerfully near in our lives. We will not know in what way God is near when our feet are tired and the outcome of a problem is uncertain. Yet we can look back on troubled moments and discover God's nearness. Cultivating the ears and eyes to hear and see the stories of God's nearness means practicing looking at our lives in retrospect. We look theologically at our autobiographies.

You may wish to take a few moments to do a simple exercise to help you discover your own life as a resource for stories. Select one of the following for meditation: A time in your life when you wandered aimlessly and found purpose, when you were lonely and someone came to you, when you were afraid and someone lent you courage, or when you were burdened with guilt and received forgiveness. Now remember your life's story. You can play it back quickly, much like a cassette player on rewind. When an episode goes by that connects to the topic you picked, stop the rewinding of the memory tape. Now carefully relive that moment. When was it? Where was it? Who was involved? What happened? Why did your memory select this episode? You have now discovered a story of good news that comes out of your life. You may even want to write your story. Your faith autobiography, a theological retrospective on your experiences of grace, is a rich thread in personal renewal and may be woven into the stories that renew your congregation.

Our stories are old; as old as children asking, "How come . . ." on a desert three thousand years ago. Our stories are new; as new as your spouse's good-morning kiss or the smile of a child. Our stories are from far; as far as a village preacher in Africa. Our stories are near; as near as the friends in your church who know you well enough to talk when it is right to talk and just to be there when it is right just to be there.

Power is stored in those old-new, far-near stories, power enough to revitalize the congregations of mainline churches. As we hear and tell stories, we are renewed. We bring hope and vitality to our congregations. As congregations discover through stories their legacy in a history of renewal, they become renewed. As members learn to seek and discover stories, they become alert and alive to stories long ago and far away. The insight dawns, "We have a story too." In that discovery the congregation comes fascinatingly alive.

Our part in the work of revitalization is simply to spin yarns and to help others spin yarns. I do not believe that the congregations will be renewed by admonitions that only cause us to clench our teeth and try harder and feel more painfully our failures. God has given us stories. Through the centuries, the Bible story has been woven into the lives of the faithful. The weaving continues. There is plenty of yarn for weaving: stories from the Bible and the story weavers, past and present, near and far. Our call in renewing our mainline congregations is simply to discover the pattern and get on with the weaving.

As we go on together through the pages of this book, we will look for patterns of vitality that may have come to the people of God in the past. We will then discuss strategies for renewal in the congregation's life today.

Chapter 2

Discovering the Patterns

The fabric of congregational revitalization will evolve from patterns that were woven before us. Before we do our work of story weaving, we will look together to discover some of those patterns.

The denominational statistics are troubling. The Disciples of Christ have lost 25 percent of their membership in 25 years; from 1,503,004 to 1,121,301 members. Other mainline denominations report similar, alarming statistics. Those numbers represent people and worries and tears. Many congregations have fewer and fewer worshipers. Some buildings are not kept in good repair because of fewer funds or lack of interest. More congregations look to the future with concern about their ability to pay for professional pastoral leadership. Often morale is low.

At times our losses have produced spasms of guilt, fault finding, grief. At other times spasms of frantic effort erupt. Some feel morose, helpless, and hopeless. Others work hard crusading to save their church from extinction. Some may even be stoically accepting its demise.

Conversations about decline in mainline congregations often divide us into two camps. Some are sternly critical. We blame denominational leaders, seminaries, liberal theology, pastors, bishops, the hymnbook, social action, the ecumenical movement, and educational materials. This list goes on. Others of us, out of love for the church, try to discourage critical comments.

Adlai Stevenson criticized the Democratic Party when he was its presidential nominee in the 1950s. Some party loyalists tried to discourage Governor Stevenson from being critical. Stevenson replied, "Things have come to a pretty pass when a man can't cudgel his own jackass!"

I can hear the critics reply to those who would dissuade them. "It's my church too. I care for the church. It's a sorry state of affairs when someone can't cudgel his or her own jackass!"

For a moment let's venture mistreating our own jackass as we look for patterns in what is happening to our congregations. Something good may even surprise us in the patterns we discover. In fact, some of us intentionally look to our past to gain perspective in a time of uncertainty.

MOBILE POPULATION

Look to the loom of the past and see what patterns have been woven before us. One repeated pattern is that the location of our congregations stays one step behind our mobile population. The European population on the East coast produced the restless people who started the movement westward. The church had to follow its people.

The open country and small towns of the United States and Canada became well supplied with congregations. Then came the movement of people to the cities. The church has been less successful in following its people to the cities. Now the population shifts southward and westward. Mainline churches work hard to build congregations in areas of growing population. Yet, many members are lost in the transition. Many of the congregations "back home" are declining.

If our people would move as congregational units, we could revive the tabernacle used by our ancestors in the Exodus. We move as families, not as clans and communities. A pattern develops of the church losing members because it can't keep up with its mobile members.*

LOSS OF PURPOSE

A second pattern can be characterized as loss of a passionate purpose. Our purpose historically has been propelled by the urge to conquer new frontiers. One of our great myths is played on the stage of the frontier. The noble-souled European yeoman was

---

*Recommended resource: "The Movin' Family" packet by Peter M. Morgan, available from Christian Board of Publication, P.O. Box 179, St. Louis, MO 63166.

intrigued by America. Men and women were lured to the adventure of new beginnings in a "New England." They settled the eastern seaboard of North America. Their children were the next group of players to come on stage in the American frontier myth. They were intrigued by the great American wilderness. It was foreboding and forbidding. Its dark secrets, its dangers held a compelling fascination. The need to go to the wilderness, to know the wilderness and to subdue it and conquer it and to harvest its riches drove the scouts westward. Soon after came the trappers, settlers, trading-post keepers, and missionaries and preachers.

The North American church's passionate purpose has been formed in some part by the wilderness myth of America. The church's version of the wilderness myth was our passion to evangelize the North American frontier. The church of my family, the Disciples, was born on the frontier. It embodies that American myth and character. We have valued freedom, independence, the passion to evangelize, and the creation of new communities, new unities, in new settings. We still are characterized by new forms of those mythic values. We celebrate and encourage responsible freedom. Independence has matured into a covenantal polity. The creation of new communities, new unities, continues in our persistence and sacrificial efforts in ecumenism.

The mutually energizing encounter of the American wilderness myth and the Christian visions of ecumenism and evangelism produced "prairie-fire growth." My great grandfather became a Disciples preacher in 1883. He was part of the effort that caused the Disciples to grow from 400,000 to 1,200,000 members between 1875 and 1900. Methodist circuit-rider preachers, Quaker meeting houses, Episcopal missionaries to the Indians and the stories of nineteenth-century America in other denominations are all symbols of the church's participation in the frontier myth. We were a people with a passionate purpose.

About the time the North American frontier was closing, a new wilderness, a new frontier beckoned to us. The intriguing, foreboding wilderness of foreign lands captured our passion. Around the beginning of the twentieth century, we gave ourselves to winning the world for Christ in one generation. Our passion for this new wilderness to conquer focused before us a clear purpose and animated us into decisive, confident action.

A pattern is clear. When we have a new frontier to lure us and to stir our imaginations, we move with a passionate purpose. In recent years the passion is less intense, the purpose is less clear. We have re-examined the compulsion to conquer and are rightly less imperial in our outlook. We have also seen the success of our passion. The strength of institutional Christianity in America is unrivaled any place in the world. The success of the world missionary movement means that now our children in the faith in other lands, to their credit, have matured and are to be treated as adults, partners and equals. We have no new frontier. We no longer have any compulsion to conquer anything. We have lost any passionate purpose.

We could now sit in our rocking chairs and reminisce on our successes in grandmotherly satisfaction. Many of us, however, are restless for a new purpose, a new passion. We are no longer in the conquering business. Yet, we are still called to discover God's purpose for us and to be faithful in its pursuit. One important factor in congregational revitalization is the work on mission and ministry identification and action.*

BETWEEN ERAS

A third pattern is discovered by looking at the broad sweep of historical eras. We are at the end of the historical era called the Age of Reason. It began about 1600 and closed about the middle of this century. The Greek love of learning was revived and cultivated in the European cultural centers. Great rationalistic systems and structures have dominated the way our society thought, organized communal life, developed tools and manufacturing operations, thought about economic systems and expressed itself culturally. Those systems have been expressed in Cartesian philosophy, Newtonian physics, nationalism in government, capitalism and communism in economics, the symphony in music and denominationalism in Christianity. Those systems born in the previous era are likely to be radically rethought and possibly altered in a transition to a new time. Susanne K. Langer describes our transition as a violent passage.

"We live, today, in an anxious world. Later generations will probably see our age as a time of transition from one social order to

---

*Recommended resource: "Congregational Mission and Ministry Development Manual" by John R. Foulkes, available from Department of Evangelism and Membership, P.O. Box 1986, Indianapolis, IN 46206.

30

another . . . We feel ourselves swept along in a violent passage, from a world we cannot salvage to one we cannot see; and most people are afraid."[6]

The decline of the mainline denominations may be a sign of the disintegration of the era we cannot salvage. Our ambivalent responses may be due to the lack of focus on the era that is not yet to the point of being clearly seen.

The future shape of Christianity is not yet fully developed. However, the present change of the churches in relationship to society can be seen. Three institutions in society have assembled large groups of persons and families and have influenced values, direction, and focus of goals for life. These institutions have given us direction and power through myth, story, cultic and cultural expression. Those three institutions, until recently, have been liberal higher education on one side, evangelical Christianity on the other, and mainline Christianity in the middle. Mainline Christianity has shared some of the language and symbols and cultic practices with evangelical Christianity. Liberal-arts education and mainline denominational Christianity have shared a nondogmatic, free and open quest for truth. With each passing year of the last quarter century, the middle gathering point has become less and less influential. A picture suggesting this action is a three-pole circus tent with the main center pole falling in slow motion.

The pattern of life and death of eras may help us experience our situation with hope. A long-term ecumenical vision takes us beyond denominational Christianity. We may experience the death of denominations. But the pattern of changing eras helps us believe that our pain is the pain of travail. We are mothers giving life to a new church for a new time.

LIFE PHASES

This look at the loom on which we will weave the stories of renewal reveals a fourth pattern. The pattern helps us locate our congregation and our denominational family in a model of life phases. Are we in infancy or old age or somewhere in between?

I am borrowing quite freely from the work of Management Design, Inc. to help us see this pattern. A line of country music goes, "The shoes may be borrowed but the holes are mine." I borrowed the model, but I made the "holes" myself.

Institutions have life cycles. Rather than conception, gestation, birth, etc., institutional life cycles are divided into the five following periods: foundation, expansion, stabilization, breakdown, and critical. (See Figure 1.)

Fig. 1.

FOUNDATION PERIOD	EXPANSION PERIOD	STABILIZATION PERIOD	BREAKDOWN PERIOD	CRITICAL PERIOD

The *foundation period* centers around the visions of the founders. That vision critiques the present, appropriates the past, and offers a compelling image of the future. The vision has power enough to gather followers who work toward the fruition of the vision.

The *expansion period* begins the institutionalizing process. Issues faced are formation of belief systems, polity, cultic practices, lines of authority, and procedures for perpetuation.

The *stabilization period* may last a century or more but may be as brief as fifty years. The purpose of the institution is self-evident and the institution is competent in accomplishing its purpose. The need to improve is not pursued as basic change but rather as doing better what is already being done to fulfill the vision of the founders.

The *breakdown period* is marked by decline and the dismantling of structures and belief systems. There is resulting stress, doubt, and disillusionment regarding the institution's relevance and ability to adapt to its new situation. Often internal conflict occurs among members. Clarity and attention to a common purpose are lost. Old techniques are often attempted with fresh vigor but these problem-solving techniques become increasingly ineffective.

The *critical period* occurs when there is absolute doubt about the value and viability of the institution. Three outcomes are possible from this crisis point: extinction, minimal survival, or revitalization.

Do you know the history of your congregation? Where would you place it in the life cycle? Possibly it has been through the life cycle numerous times. Something or someone gives it new life, new birth, revitalization. Where in the life cycle is your congregation now?

Fig. 2.

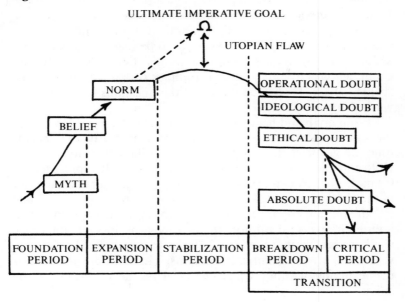

Used by permission of Management Design,
Inc. of Cincinnati, Ohio.

The vitality curve is a helpful way to understand the pattern of development and decline. (See Figure 2.) Notice that the curve has an ascending side and a descending side or a developing time and a declining time. The curve begins over the foundation period. That time in a group's life is characterized with the word "myth." Myths are the stories that capture the meaning of life. They are the lens through which a community understands itself and its calling. Note here the importance of stories, the focal point of this book, for beginnings. Stories recollect and celebrate the coming together into community for common pursuit of a shared purpose. The resources of the past are used in the present to move toward a common vision of the future. Do you know the stories of the founders of your congregation? Your denomination?

The term after "myth" that characterizes the next institutional life phase is "belief." Myth powers a group. Belief points a group. Precision of language is worked out in defining who the group is, how it is to relate to the world about it, how members are to relate to each other, how choices are to be made for the group's actions. In my own denomination, the Disciples, Alexander Campbell was a young enough founder to live and lead in the "belief" phase. He helped work out the questions of belief in his work *Christian Systems*.

From myth and belief the group moves to "norm." Norms are the stable patterns of expectations and actions. In the "norm" time the group is moving toward the fulfillment of its purpose. Notice at the top of the curve an omega sign. It represents the ultimate goal. A gap exists between the omega sign and the peak of the vitality curve. That gap can be labeled many ways: original sin, the human condition, incapacity for sustained development, failure. In every institution there comes the loss of innocence when we realize that the ideal will not be attained. The ultimate vision will always eventually elude us. That loss of innocence is the beginning of doubt, which characterizes the decline side of the curve.

When doubt comes, it is first at the operational level. Old methods and strategies no longer seem to be working as well as previously in moving the group toward its vision. The group may intensify its efforts trying to make the old ways work, or may go looking for new programs and techniques.

A deeper level of breakdown emerges as ideological doubt. The myths of the group may now be only vaguely understood but are basically trusted. The group is challenging the intellectual assumptions that underlie the organization.

Doubt reaches deepest at the ethical level. When a group is troubled by its own basic myths and beliefs, it is experiencing ethical doubt. It happens in congregations when a family questions whether it is "good" or "God's will" for them to belong to this congregation any longer. They are in ethical doubt.

If the downward movement continues, a group reaches absolute doubt. The group's survival is in jeopardy. It may die. A few may remain and delay the group's death. Or, a new founding phase calls together a new and/or renewed group that begins ascending again the vitality curve.

As we develop strategies for revitalization in our congregations, we can learn from the vitality curve and institutional life phases. Institutions can engage in building their own histories. When the institution is on the decline side of the vitality curve, when it is experiencing doubt, it has begun to admit that the institution is unsatisfactory to many people. The honesty in that painful admission may be a first step on the pathway to transformation. It allows the institution to live openly with contradiction, experimentation, and searching. People in the institution need to be comfortable with error and failure. It is a time of trial and error and learning and correcting from the errors. Groups in the institution need to learn to be error-embracing in order to gain insight rather than error-denying. In the searching and the contradictions, hope begins to grow. The desire for the not-yet is rekindled.

One learning is that our congregations have an energy-building side and an energy-using side. Story, belief clarification, mission, and goal setting create energy. The living out of the myth, belief, mission is depleting. We who lead in congregations need to balance the exhorting of people to greater commitment, an energy-depleting act, with moments of song and story and sharing deep tenets of faith and forming a common vision of the future, an energy-building act. In those energy-building acts the congregation is restored and refreshed. They are then able to spend themselves in hard, painful, doubt-creating, sometimes disillusioning acts of ministry.

A second learning is the importance of dealing with doubts at all levels. Programs are tools. They are means or ways of doing mission. They need to be always evaluated and refined. Operational doubt is a healthy contributor to our congregation's effectiveness. However, programs are not magic. The problems of renewal cannot be solved by starting a new "Pony Express" campaign or a new teacher-training course. Doubt must be dealt with at all levels.

Ideological doubt, honestly and lovingly faced, can contribute to the congregation's revitalization. Thoughtful discussion on what we believe about God, the church, our personal vocation, our group's reason for life, gives the congregation a plumb line by which constantly to see its actions and to fine-tune them into compatibility with belief. Operational doubt causes us to ask, "Is it effective?" Ideological doubt causes us to ask, "Is it faithful?"

Ethical doubt can take us to the heart of revitalization. We enter here the realm of spirituality. Dealing with ethical doubts takes us to the source of our energy and vision. We examine what is "good" for our congregation as we prayerfully reflect on and tell again the stories of sacred history in Scripture and Tradition.

The mainline congregations are in a time of serious need for revitalization. Liturgy and matters of the Spirit are of first importance, especially at this time of need for institutional revitalization. It is a time of going back to the basic activities that animated our founders. In the foundation phase of our institution the leaders and people are in touch with an animating myth that causes them to assess their present situation, envision a new future, and propose the use of the materials of the past to build that future. If our congregations today are to create the foundation for revitalized life, it is time to cultivate gifts for the encounter with God as we assess our present times and use the resources of the past, Scripture and Tradition, to envision our new future. In short, it is time to see the burning bush and to hear the still small voice.

We cannot go where God has not already been. No matter where our congregation goes on the vitality curve, God awaits as we open and pray over our Bible. In the foundation phase of our institutional life, God awaits us in the stories of Creation and Pentecost. In the expansion phase, God meets us in the stories of Moses on the mountain and his consultation with Jethro on ways to organize and bring order to newly freed slaves. In the stabilization period God meets us in the stories of Jesus' praising the widow's offering and Paul's teaching the Corinthians about gifts. God awaits us in the breakdown times. We hear God entering our story as we ponder moments of transition in Scripture: The Exodus, the Exile, the disillusionment of the followers of Jesus after the Crucifixion. God even awaits as we face the possibility of the death of our congregation. We cry out in pain in the prayers of The Psalms. We deal with the themes of death and the hope of resurrection as we hear again the story of Jesus' death and resurrection. No matter where our congregation takes us in the phases of life, we are never alone. God awaits us in the sacred stories.

The book *Shaping the Coming Age of Religious Life* gives theological perspective to the life cycle model.

". . . religious life . . . [is] a charism within the Church, that is, . . . a gift of God's spirit given for the good of the whole people of God. This inbreaking and movement of the Spirit in history manifests a mysterious pattern of life and growth, death and dying—and rebirth. To give specificity to this pattern of life, death and resurrection, a historical model for the evaluation of religious life as a movement within the Church . . . [is] presented. . . ."[7]

A STORY

Part of the strategy of revitalization is to return to the foundation stories, a reconnecting to life-giving Tradition. Tradition is the cumulative experience of the church under the power and guidance of the Holy Spirit. Tradition is a God-given resource for our vitality. One way to acquire the stories of founding is to read the biographies from the early history of your denomination. Look especially for prayerful people, persons gifted in spirituality. You may find the richest gifts of this kind in the lives of the less well known. I discovered the following story in my own Disciples of Christ heritage. In the telling of the story I attempt to weave the story of Dr. Robert Richardson into the story of congregational renewal.[8]

A Founder for Our Future

A major portion of the formation of our destiny is suggested by some holy ground, "nigh unto Bethany," West Virginia, at Bethphage. Bethphage was a small farm on high ground with a magnificent view of Buffalo Creek and the village of Bethany. The master of that farm 130 years ago was Dr. Robert Richardson. He was the local physician, professor, and bursar of Bethany College, an editor of the "Millennial Harbinger," tireless worker in the Stone-Campbell movement, elder at the Bethany Church and counselor to Alexander Campbell.

Richardson's life calls us to a fresh awareness of spirituality.

Cloyd Goodnight and Dwight Stevenson point to this spirituality in Richardson's biography as they describe the relationship between Campbell and Richardson.

. . . they made a good team. Campbell was a great student of the arts and religion, a powerful religious statesman with real sagacity, while

Robert Richardson was a keen student of science and religion, a quiet thinker, and a retiring but firm adviser. Both recognized that they worked well together. One was the advocate, while the other was the counselor. Their cooperation was not a result of sameness; it was rather a harmony of difference. One was coldly intellectual; the other was warmly devotional, almost mystical. . . . Richardson was always more nearly a mystic than any other of the pioneer Disciples.[9]

The picture we get of Richardson is of a diligent, disciplined man who guarded his time of devotion, silence, and solitude. He pulled away to his own separate home, away from the village. He had his study. After the evening meal the family would pray together and sing together, often with Dr. Richardson playing the violin or flute. He left those domestic concerts early to go to his study. With the soft, happy sounds of music in the background, Richardson studied, thought, meditated and prayed.

Around the Bethany countryside 130 years ago Dr. Richardson, astride his horse, Barney, was a familiar sight as he went to and from Bethany or made house calls on his patients. He did not like carriages. They made him "seasick." In fact, sometimes he would take the carriages sent by well-meaning patients and become sick himself on an errand of trying to make someone else well!

Wherever Richardson went, he carried his "common sense" book. Those who practice the spiritual life today are frequently advised to keep a journal. Dr. Richardson's "common sense" book was a journal of his time in solitude on horseback. Tidbits of that journal of life in the Spirit have enriched the church as they appeared in articles in *The Millennial Harbinger*.

He insisted, for example, on spirituality as a balance to Campbell's rationalism, not as opposition to it. The lack of the beauty of Christ within Christians, he wrote, makes us "clouds without rain, trees that bear no fruit, failing fountains, which mock the thirsty traveler."[10]

Richardson is a witness to the possibilities of vitality through difficulty. That witness is important to our era in the church as it seeks revitalization in a time of doubt. His life was not total peace and harmony. His coming to the Campbells caused a severe rupture in his relationship with his Episcopalian father. He had to overcome his natural timidity and reserve if he was to become a public speaker and thereby a leader of the church he loved. His spiritual orientation sometimes brought him into conflict with the older Alexander Campbell. Mr. Campbell was a formidable and intimidating opponent. We can imagine the conflicts at times being good-natured. Mr. Campbell spoke of Richardson's addiction to metaphors. Other times the conflict became public and rocked the church. Tolbert Fanning, president of Franklin College in Tennessee, managed to drive the wedge of misunderstanding deep between Campbell and Richardson by creating the suspicion that Richardson was opposing Campbell with a "spirit only" approach to faith.

Possibly Richardson's heaviest burden was a physical problem of weak eyes. There would be episodes when he could not write or even read. Sometimes his eyes would have to be rested for days or weeks. In the most extreme case Richardson could not use his eyes for close work for two years.

Through all of these discouraging times Richardson again and again received the new life that God poured back into him. He became reconciled with his father. He became a speaker, though of halting style, whose prose had the essence of poetry. He cleared up the misunderstanding with Campbell and even received his public apology. In the temporary times of disability, he made good use of readers and secretaries. His eyesight kept coming back.

No wonder Robert Richardson, Disciple of the Spirit, is like a fresh fountain of cold stream-water to us who thirst for revitalization. He brings us, a people who believe through knowledge, the richness of life in the Spirit. He lets us discover that knowledge is only one rung in the ladder of communion with God.

The heritage we receive from Campbell and Richardson is a balance of faith through knowing and faith through the Spirit. That balance of reason and spirituality is best portrayed in a scene described by J. W. McGarvey. "The richest service of all [at the Bethany Church] was when they had a sermon by Mr. Campbell followed by Dr. Richardson . . . at the Lord's Table." Dwight Stevenson observes in Richardson's biography that no high priest ever entered the holy of holies with more reverence than did Dr. Richardson enter upon his duties on these occasions.[11]

We have looked to the past in preparation for learning more about story weaving as a means of revitalizing congregations. We have discovered patterns in the decline and revitalization of congregations. Mobile population is a pattern of decline as is the loss of a passionate purpose. A pattern can be seen in living beyond a time we cannot salvage and a future time we cannot yet see. The life cycle of institutions teaches us we need to return constantly to the realm of spirituality. In returning to resources of prayer and story from Scripture and Tradition, we will look further for patterns.

GOD'S PERSISTENCE

Urban Holmes in *Turning to Christ* helps us understand the biblical promise of renewal.

> . . . renewal, *properly understood*, is the community's response, in grace, to the Gospel, the proclamation that God's reign is upon us. Renewal is God shaping our vision and action. For the people of God, renewed by the Spirit of Christ, their world is turned upside down. The renewed community no longer constitutes its world of meaning as the society closed to God. It "marches to the sound of a different drummer."[12] . . . the word for "renewal" . . . is found in various forms—*anakainoo, ananeoomai,* and *anakainizo*—in the Hebrews, Titus, and Pauline letters. Paul writes, "But be you transformed by the renewal of the mind" (Romans 12:2; Holmes). The mind pertains to the inner person. Paul says elsewhere that renewal has to do with a change within (2 Corinthians 4:16). How does this change occur? One answer is given by the author of Titus, who writes that Christ has saved us "through the bath that brings about regeneration and through the renewal by the Holy Spirit" (Titus 3:5; Holmes). It is the same point made by the Fourth Evangelist (John 3:5). Baptism is the effective sign of renewal, if not the exclusive occasion of the continuing gift of the Spirit. . . . If one is to respond to the good news that the reign of God is at hand, then the mind must be transformed, so that we are open to the Spirit, who teaches us the truth in Christ—the truth that will make us free.[13]

One day the biblical promise of revitalization came to me in story form. I had heard Elton Trueblood speak publicly since I was a child in the 1940s. A few years ago I was to sit with him and a few colleagues for a private consultation on church renewal. Dr.

Trueblood has now reached the phase of his life when he can be called a sage. As he sat listening to us and speaking to us, he seemed the very personification of God's enduring wisdom and hope. He affirmed that God reaches for his people to offer them life as persistently as the ocean waves come to the beach. Listen to the repeated promise of life coming time and time again throughout the Bible. "The people who walked in darkness have seen a great light" (Isaiah 9:2). Sometimes the night of discouragement can seem to last forever. But, the morning is coming. God reaches for God's people to offer life. ". . . can these bones live? . . . these bones are the whole house of Israel. Behold, they say, 'Our bones are dried up, and our hope is lost; we are clean cut off. . . .' I will put my Spirit within you, and you shall live . . ." (Ezekiel 37:3, 11, 14). Sometimes our congregations just seem to lie lifeless, like old bones. Then time and time again something will stir and rustle about. Someone in the church moves a little. The old bones begin to move, then to walk, then to dance. God reaches to God's people to offer life. ". . . I will raise up the booth of David that is fallen and repair its breaches, and raise up its ruins, and rebuild it as in the days of old" (Amos 9:11). Mix the mortar. Stir the paint. Company is coming. God reaches to God's people to offer life. ". . . you, child, will be called the prophet of the Most High; for you will go before the Lord to prepare his ways . . . through the tender mercy of our God . . . the day shall dawn upon us from on high to give light to those who sit in darkness and in the shadow of death, to guide our feet into the way of peace" (Luke 1:76, 78-79). Among us come those who, like John the Baptist, let us know the dayspring from above has visited. God reaches again and again, as persistently as the waves coming to the beach, to offer us new life. The pattern is clear: God is persistent!

The biblical story portrays a pattern of God's people coming to many times when it was necessary to make a shift in the way they perceived reality and related to that reality. They made those paradigm shifts. We may be in a time of paradigm shift for mainline congregations. We are part of a continuing saga of life in transition, being renewed.

One of those times of paradigm shift was the Exodus. Rolland Pfile, a friend and colleague in the Division of Homeland Ministries, has a delightful version of the Exodus paradigm shift. He calls it . . .

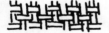

Can YHWH Grow Corn?

When the Israelites came wandering in from the wilderness and conquered and settled Canaan, they experienced a shift in how they saw life and how they functioned. They knew YHWH was mighty in battle, could provide manna in the wilderness, could give the law to govern their lives, and could guide them by a fiery pillar. But now they were becoming city folks and farmers. Could YHWH grow corn!?

How do you grow corn? First you watch a Canaanite. You learn that you dig a hole, throw seed in it, kick the earth over it, water it, and go consort with the prostitutes of Ba'al. All steps seem necessary.

Workshops and seminars were offered to all the twelve tribes of Israel. The people were dutifully taking notes: 1. Dig a hole; 2. Throw in corn; 3. Kick dirt over it; 4. Water it; 5. Consort with the . . . what? But YHWH is a jealous God. Yes, but can YHWH grow corn?

We gain much by being a people with a faith that has developed through many centuries. We gain the assurance that God, and our faith in God, is always much greater than our perception of God. More discoveries await us. A new paradigm will emerge. God is able to grow corn!

A paradigm shift also occurred during the reign of King Josiah. We find his story told in the twenty-second and twenty-third chapters of 2 Kings.

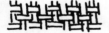

It Looked Impossible

Recall what young King Josiah faced. His people were proud of their great Davidic tradition. But, in fact, the kingdom of Saul, David, and Solomon was now only a token of its former self. The kingdom had split into North and South, and the North was completely destroyed, gone. The southern territory was mainly Jerusalem and a little more. The people had been ruled at times by kings who would seek faithfulness to YHWH. Josiah's grandfather Hezekiah was one of these. They had also been ruled by kings who supported the local deity Ba'al or when it was politically advantageous, the gods of the superpowers like Assyria. Josiah's own father, Manasseh, was one of these.

Josiah's political situation was impossible. He was the thumb between the hammer and the nailhead of Egypt and Assyria. To make things more complicated Babylon, a new superpower, was on the rise and would soon dominate that world. In the terms of the other patterns we have seen, Judah and King Josiah lived in a time between eras. They were in the breakdown or critical part of their history.

It is in this situation that our story unfolds. Using the pretext of temple repairs, the priests "found" a hidden book of the covenant. In all probability they had hidden it there themselves when Josiah's father was on the throne. They waited until this moment when young Josiah came of age to "find" it and present it to their king.

The king had the book read and interpreted by a prophetess. He then tore his clothes in grief as he learned the extent of his ancestors' unfaithfulness to YHWH. He had the book publicly read, and instituted a major reform.

Josiah was not in an easy position. He had to fear Ashurbanipal, the Assyrian. And yet, he was more afraid of the wrath of the Lord than he was of the displeasure of the Assyrian king. Josiah gave his people at least four things. 1. These people, who saw themselves as tumbling out of control, were given a frame of reference for what was happening to them. It is called the Deuteronomic cycle of history. When we serve God, we prosper. When we fail to serve God, we suffer. 2. These people, whose identity was linked to their great King David, were pointed to a new spiritual founder. They became the people of Moses again. 3. These people, who were frequently the victims of more powerful nations, were given an enduring base for their existence that was stronger than political and military might. They became a people of the law, a people of the Book. 4. These people, who had little reason to hope, were given hope. Those who cry to the Lord are constantly offered new life. Yes, they would be conquered by Babylon and exiled. But in Moses, in that book, in that hope were the seeds that rebuilt Jerusalem and Judaism and Judaism's child, Christianity, which are alive today when signs of Babylon's might are only mute artifacts in today's museums.

The loom upon which we will do the work of congregational renewal reveals many patterns. The church has a pattern of being behind its people when they relocate into new areas of the country. With the closing of the American frontier and the maturing of churches around the world, a new purpose has not captured our passion for an enduring time. We have seen a pattern of being in a time between eras. Also, we have discovered some patterns of aging. Congregations, like any living being, go from a birth date to a death date. The stories from Tradition and Scripture also reveal a pattern. Even when life is in transition, when a paradigm shift is occurring, God persistently reaches toward God's people and offers life.

HUNGER FOR RELIGIOUS EXPERIENCE

We may be living in a time of a paradigm shift in mainline congregations. People in our congregations now express a hunger for vital, authentic religious experiences. They come to church with an innate longing to experience the presence of God. They believe that such experiences are possible and that they give joy, meaning, and guidance to life. In recent years many have left our mainline congregations with the hunger unfilled.

John Biersdorf comments on our longing for the experience of God's presence in *Hunger for Experience*.

". . . people do not seek theological talk about how one can discuss the experience of God. They hunger for the actual *presence* of God . . . one has to have experience before guides and judgments about experience make any sense. . . . Theory is not an end in itself, but a means to more faithful practice. . . . People today hunger for the experience of reality out of which life's meaning may come, not for *discussion* of reality."[14]

Our prayer of longing sings in minor key with the psalmists, "O God, thou art my God, I seek thee, my soul thirsts for thee; my flesh faints for thee, as in a dry and weary land where no water is" (Psalm 63:1). "As a hart longs for flowing streams, so longs my soul for thee, O God. My soul thirsts for God, for the living God. When shall I come and behold the face of God? My tears have been my food day and night, while men say to me continually, 'Where is your God?'" (Psalm 42:1-3).

Abraham Maslow has done some pioneering work in the field of inner experience. He interviewed persons who were gifted in fulfilling their life's promise. He discovered among these "self-actualizing" persons what he called "peak experiences"; i.e., experiences that confirm connectedness with all life in which each person or thing is enjoyed and cherished for its own sake. Peak experiences bring both feelings of humility and power. Persons with these experiences are open to reality, not personally threatened by it. Self-actualizing persons are characterized by peak experiences, experiences of the transcendent. The residue of those experiences produces a sensitivity to pain and suffering, which can be faced and ministered to because of the overarching experience of the unity and goodness of life and one's place in it.

The expressed hunger for religious experience is a clue that our congregations are undergoing a paradigm shift, a change in the pattern of how reality is perceived and life is lived in relationship to reality. Let's look at the dominant pattern of congregational life in the last few decades.

All churches have characteristic traits, which we can describe with four biblical terms. The churches have *koinonia*. This is the biblical word that translates as "fellowship." Its full meaning is that we are with each other as partakers and participants in the life of Christ.

The churches have *didache*. That word translates into "teaching." We are teaching and learning in our Sunday schools, our women's and men's fellowship groups, special leader-training events, "Minute for Mission" talks, etc.

The churches have *kerygma*. *Kerygma* means "the proclamation." It is preaching. It is both the acts of sharing the Christian story and the content of that story. It is the Good News and the proclaiming of the Good News.

The churches have *diakonia*. That word in English is "service" or "ministry." The good works we do in the name of Christ are included in the term. Money for the hungry in Africa, or going in to paint the home of a shut-in member is *diakonia*.

In each congregation we will find varying amounts of all four biblical ingredients. Some churches, for example, may have little *kerygma* (proclamation), but a lot of *didache* (teaching), and be about average in *koinonia* (fellowship) and *diakonia* (service). In fact, if we look closely, we will find one of the four ingredients dominates. That dominant aspect of church life is the conscious or unconscious reason why the people think that congregation exists. The dominant ingredient will have the other three as subordinate. They will function primarily to serve the dominant trait.

My observation is that *koinonia* has been the base or primary factor in the majority of mainline congregations for the last two generations.

Let me recollect my experience of what is probably the most prevalent pattern. I was pastor for ten years of a *koinonia* (fellowship)-based congregation. That was reflected in the closeness and caring of members for each other. They liked to stay after church and visit. They were in each other's homes. Outsiders' most frequent comment was, "Your people really love each other." I quickly learned, though, that all other ingredients were subordinate. One year a bridge club was highly successful, while a new Bible study didn't get off the ground. *Koinonia* won over *didache*.

Probably the most clear picture I got of this was the time I was doing everything I could to have our worship be as fresh and innovative as possible. Dullness was a sin to me. I was enthusiastically talking to one of the members, trying to convince him how good this was. He responded, "Preacher, you can do what you want, I come here for the people." Even though he was disgruntled about the worship it did not matter much. The primary reason for the church for him was intact. It was *koinonia*.

The *koinonia*-based congregation does many good things. Being with people who care deeply for each other is to receive a great gift. To continue my story, we had some success in bringing together small groups. But, subordinate traits had to serve the dominant trait of *koinonia*. Group participants needed something to do together. Some time was spent in study (*didache*). Other small groups participated in work trips to poor communities of Appalachia and collecting and loading large truckloads of materials for poor people in other parts of the country (*diakonia*). These activities were subordinate to *koinonia*.

In many of our congregations the pattern is changing. (See Figure 3.) People are expressing their hunger for experiencing the presence of God. That expressed longing is in many congregations a basic shift in the dominant value of our churches' life. We now have the opportunity to lead and participate in moving *kerygma* into the dominant position in the churches. We may now weave the yarns of the biblical story into our personal stories

46

Fig. 3.

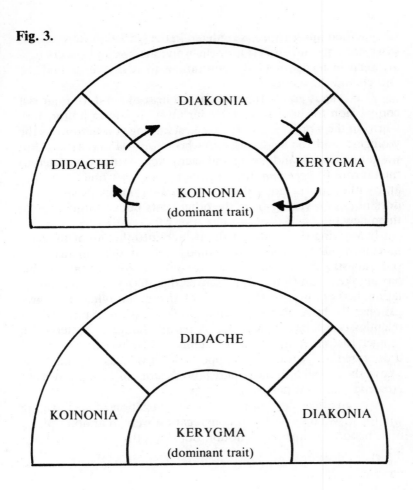

in such a way that our stories, and those of our congregations, will be transformed.

The *koinonia* is good. Fellowship makes life pleasant. But, fellowship unleavened by *kerygma* runs the risk of making the church the country club of the modestly affluent.

The *didache* is good. To teach and learn expands the horizons of human vision. But, without the biblical story our teaching is sterile dogma or pious platitudes.

When *kerygma* is dominant, then our teaching is not reduced in importance but becomes the all-important learning of God's story. When our learning is centered in the Christian story, God's story becomes our story. Our beliefs and actions and experiences are seen in terms of God's continuing to re-create us and the church and the world.

Diakonia is good. To serve friends near at hand, to pour out compassion to those who suffer far away, has been honored by Christ in the words ". . . let the greatest among you become as the youngest, and the leader as one who serves" (Luke 22:26). But when our serving and giving and sacrificing are not connected to the taproot of *kerygma*, the Christian story, how quickly we tire and wither in our good deeds. When *kerygma* is dominant, it does not drain vitality from the other traits but continually gives them new life.

In weaving the stories of the church into the life of the congregation and its members, we come to a loom that already has a rich tapestry framed and ready for our artistic endeavors. We have looked at the loom and discovered patterns: a mobile population, loss of purpose, the passing of an era, the aging of congregations. We have also discovered God's life-giving Spirit, which relentlessly reaches to offer life. A recent change in pattern, the hunger for religious experience, hints that now may be one of those rare times when a fresh opportunity awaits us. We may now weave the gospel into the congregation's story in such a way as to create vibrant new designs of vitality.

We can affect the destiny of our congregations if we have the will for it. We may wish our congregation were in another phase in its history. A time of less doubt. But *this* is the time we are born into.

 ### Mrs. Miller's Pies

As a child I remember Mrs. Miller, who kept waiting for her husband to buy her a new cook stove. She had an old coal burner. Her neighbor's new range looked awfully good to her.

She kept talking about pies, "fixin' pies for my kids, homemade pies." Her husband never got around to buying a new stove. Her kids grew up and voted before they got homemade pie! She missed the moment of feeding her children homemade pie.

We are to live and work fully and faithfully in the times we are given, and not wait until things get right.

The Unfired Rifle

A family went house hunting in New England a few years ago. They came across an old colonial home that had been in the same family since it was built. They were immediately interested in it.

An old rifle hung over the fireplace; the prospective buyer asked the owner if it had been used in the Revolutionary War. She answered with this story.

"The rifle was never fired. You see old Uncle Zeb couldn't work up much enthusiasm for that little revolution. Oh, he was a strong patriot all right. But he had a picture of a neatly uniformed company of soldiers with brass buttons and polished weapons marching to his door and a messenger reading an official announcement from General Washington commissioning him to command that company. He dreamed of the day he would take his place in the march of destiny commanding men as they drove out the British and formed a new nation.

"What happened, in reality, was a rag-tag group of farmers rode up and yelled through the window, 'Hey, Zeb, there's a hell of a fight goin' on up at Concord. Git your gun and let's go.' Uncle Zeb couldn't work up much enthusiasm for that kind of little revolution, and he missed it. He missed contributing to the building of his own dream. The rifle has never been fired."

How will we build our future? It won't happen as we imagine it. Yet, God is still offering us *this* moment in history. It is our time to reach out and receive the yarns of new life offered by God from Scripture, Tradition, and contemporary life.

How will we build our future? Let me paraphrase Robert Richardson. In our union with Christ we will be clouds with life-giving rain, trees with luscious fruits and fountains of cold stream-water for thirsty travelers.

We have seen the pattern. We must now get on with the weaving.

Chapter 3

Getting Started

Our vital work of story weaving now begins. We are like weavers the first day on the job.

We have learned where to get yarn. Our stories for the warp come from the Bible. Our stories for the woof come from church tradition, the global church, the ecumenical movement, persons near to us, and our theological reflections on our autobiographies.

We discovered some patterns already woven into the loom. In the coming together of warp and woof we see God repeatedly and persistently reaching for God's people to revitalize their life. In the life phases on institutions we see a church can deplete all of its energy in ministry unless it constantly replenishes energy by returning to its myths, the stories of foundings in Scripture and Tradition. A recent pattern is seen in the hunger for religious experience. That hunger is producing a change in the church, a paradigm shift. Shared experiences of good news become the base that gives substance to the teaching and learning in the congregation, gives depth to its fellowship and restores energy and passion to its witness and service.

In this chapter we will look at a piece of "goods," the biblical story of Joseph woven into a story from the life of Pope John XXIII. We will then examine some methods of weaving and offer some guidance in using those methods. In this "how to" chapter, I have used some personal stories. As you read, take a moment now and then to identify some of your own stories that you as a leader might use. In the remaining chapters, we will seek ways to do story weaving in the congregation's life of prayer and worship, its educational programs, its fellowship and its witness and service.

How is the Christian story communicated? One obvious and important way of communicating the story is the sermon. One of the words we hear for sermon is homily. We think of a homily as a short sermon. Many Protestants think of it as the Roman Catholic term for preaching. Homily in its original use implied personal conversation. That use may give us a clue of how to recognize and share stories. Those stories respond to the hunger for authentic religious experiences of many Christians in mainline churches. Homily fits the pattern of the current paradigm shift in mainline congregations toward the *kerygma*, the hearing and sharing of the story of Good News.

Luke uses *homileo* two times in his work Luke-Acts. *Homileo* describes conversation in Luke 24:14, 17, the story of the Emmaus Road, and in Acts 20:11, the story of Paul's ministering to the boy thought dead after falling out of a window. The connotations of the term include the coming together of persons, and companionship. Clarity and appropriation of meaning and insight are gained in the context of the warmth of human relationship. In the Emmaus Road story the *homileo*, conversation, moves on to be woven into the scriptural story and later full insight is given in the breaking of bread. In the story in Acts 20, Paul preaches too long and too late. A boy drops off to sleep and accidentally falls out a window and is thought to be dead. Paul tends to the boy. The group then shares conversation, *homileo*, and the breaking of bread. Notice both stories include accounts of conversation and sharing the Eucharist. Our *homileo* is bathed in a sacramental light as we come together for mutual enrichment and insight in story sharing.

Story weaving is the interweaving of the biblical story with our own stories in such a way that life is transformed. Story weaving has in place the warp of the biblical stories. The woof of our stories shuttles back and forth into the biblical stories so that our life takes on the coloration and texture of the biblical story.

Examine the warp and woof that come together to make up the fabric of the following stories. First, the warp, a story from our ancient lore.

The Story of Two Josephs

A young man who was favored by his father became a victim of sibling rivalry. He was a dreamer. He did not help his relationship with his brothers by telling them of his dreams in which they bowed before him. His father's special gift of an amazing colored coat further alienated him from his brothers.

One day the brothers schemed to rid the family of the favored son. They sold him into slavery to a caravan that was passing through their area. They dipped his amazing colored coat in animal blood and took it to the father with the report that he had been killed.

The young man went through many adventures as a servant in the distant land of Egypt. Eventually he was falsely accused and sent to prison. In prison he interpreted the dreams of the inmates.

One of the prisoners was freed and went to work for the pharaoh. One day, the pharaoh told his staff one of his dreams. His counselors could make no sense of the dream. The former prisoner remembered the young man who interpreted dreams back in prison. He was sent for. He told the pharaoh that his dreams meant the country was about to experience seven years of prosperity followed by seven years of failing crops. The pharaoh was impressed and asked the young man's advice. The young man counseled that the plentiful time be used to store up great quantities of grain to be used during the lean time. The pharaoh was so pleased with the counsel that he named the young man "secretary of agriculture."

The years of plentiful harvests and the years of lean harvests came as the young man had predicted. Under his leadership Egypt was prepared.

Meanwhile, back at the young man's home, his family suffered famine because they did not save grain during the bountiful years. The family heard that there was grain available in Egypt. The brothers were sent on a mission to acquire grain.

In Egypt they appeared before a young important official whom they did not recognize. The official recognized his own brothers. His feelings were torn between longing for reconciliation with his brothers, rekindled anger at their betrayal years before, and the need to find out about his father. After a time of testing his brothers, the young man came down from his seat of authority, opened his arms and simply said, "I am your brother, Joseph."

Now the woof.

In 1963 a delegation of Jews was to have an audience with Pope John XXIII. As they entered the Vatican, competing feelings stirred within them. They felt respect for one of the great spiritual leaders of the world. They also felt resentment and righteous rage for the apparent silence of the Vatican in the face of the sufferings of their people in the Holocaust twenty years before.

At the meeting of Pope John XXIII and the Jews, the Pope, Angelo Giuseppe Roncalli waived aside all protocol and simply walked over to the delegation and greeted them with the words, "I am your brother, Giuseppe."

The warp of biblical story and woof of personal story were woven together. The moment was transformed.

The Pope's titles take nine lines to print. The list begins with Bishop of Rome, Vicar of Christ and ends with Servant of the Servants of God. The Pope could have been introduced by any of the nine lines of titles. But John XXIII chose to introduce himself simply by one of the names given to him at birth. Joseph, Giuseppe in Italian, is a name associated with the reconciliation of brothers by those who know the biblical story. As he spoke the name "Giuseppe," from down the centuries echoed in the halls of the Vatican the name for reconciliation. The Pope's name and story were woven into the biblical story. The moment was woven into the biblical story. The lives of the Jewish delegation and this great Christian brother were woven together. In the woven story of Joseph, Giuseppe, and the Jews, lives were transformed.

What methods can be used in congregations to help persons develop the art of seeing and hearing their own stories as part of the extended narrative of Scripture?

A simple beginning is to have persons identify the biblical character who reflects their own life situations, personal characteristics, or desired attributes. Begin by having them think silently about characters from the Bible with whom they identify. As you guide their reflections prior to the silence, suggest that they look for a person who is like them or a person who has experienced life as they have experienced it. An alternative can be silent meditation on the person they most admire in the Bible.

After two or three minutes of silence, have persons simply share the name and/or event of their biblical character. If the total group is large, then smaller groups of about four persons need to be arranged prior to the time of silence. Allow curiosity to peak on why people pick the biblical characters they do. Sometimes you will see heads nodding in instant recognition as a woman who prefers the kitchen to the parlor names Martha.

Other times you will see brows furrow as people wonder, "What is the connection between LeRoy and Daniel?" A bit of consciousness raising without words can occur when you ask for a show of hands of persons who selected male biblical characters, then female characters. It is even more interesting to see the hands of women who chose male characters and men who chose female characters. This unspoken editorial often makes it clear that all of us could be open to more Scripture and its people.

The next level of reflection and meditation moves us toward story weaving. Have the members of the group move into the silence to think about why they picked the character or event they did. Encourage each one to remember a specific incident in his or her life that is brought to mind by the biblical character or event. Have them enjoy reliving that moment in their memories: names, places, faces, dates, actions, feelings, consequences. After remembering, participants write 1. The name of their character, 2. Why they chose the character, 3. A short description of the incident they recalled, 4. Thoughts on how their story and their character's story weave together. About ten minutes is needed for the reflection and writing the journal page. Also allow about ten minutes for those who wish to share their stories with their groups of four.

A group member, Peter, named Zacchaeus as his biblical character. He then told the following story.

Two Little Men Up a Tree

"Zacchaeus, you remember, was the little man who was a tax collector who got up a tree. Jesus came calling on him and changed his life.

"Those of us who are short have what I call a 'Napoleonic complex.' The world favors tall people, but that is not going to stop us. By effort and push and determination we'll show you that we can be just as important, just as successful as any other person. The heart of Napoleon beats in most of us who are short. I heard about one short person who commented, 'I'm not short. I'm just tightly wound!' You may not like us. But, you don't ignore us or overlook us.

"I imagine Zacchaeus was that way. You may not like your tax collector, but you ignore him at your peril!

"The Napoleonic complex can 'get you up a tree.' In my case I wanted more than anything in the world to be known as a good pastor, a successful minister. That drive may have contributed to a break in health. The doctor ordered a cutback in responsibilities and activities. I was told to spend two years resting and doing minimal work. You can imagine the effect on me. I had to lie resting while my inner voice was saying, 'You have to get out there and make the church go. You have to be out there proving your worth.' It was like being cooked in my own juices.

"Into that situation Jesus came with a word of hospitality and grace. He visited Zacchaeus' home. My word of hospitality and grace came from five different elders who on five different occasions came and said in five different ways, 'Pete, we love you not because you're successful, but because you are you. Your important work for a while is taking care of you. We'll take care of the church.' That was a moment of grace. Zacchaeus was never again just another Bible story. His story was my story. And you know what else? The church never did better than it did those two years."

A second way of leading people in the congregation to do story weaving begins with a text from Scripture. This approach, like the Bible character meditation described, enters the story through prayerful silence. In the silence we are given eyes to see and ears to hear the stories. Of course, beginning with the text opens endless possibilities as opposed to the biblical character approach, which is quite limited. The biblical character is a good starting place. The next step is learning to listen to the text for its story and then to weave into it the stories of our meditations.

We read the Scripture and then let our mind and imagination look for events in our life or our ministry suggested by the text. We can then move on to remember the life stories of people we know. This method was described in Chapter One as we explored people near to us as sources of stories. It will be expanded in Chapter Four as we discuss ways of praying the Scripture.

Howard Thurman, the great black twentieth-century pastor and writer on the life of prayer, shares an example in his meditation on the disillusioned disciples after the Crucifixion (John 21:1-14). The text and Thurman's meditation are good yarn for weaving into our stories as we seek congregational renewal.

55

After the crucifixion one of the disciples said, "Well, I'm going fishing." The event outside the city wall seemed to have exhausted the possibility of life and of God, to have made of him who died on the cross its prisoner. Later these disciples had another kind of experience that completely changed their feelings. . . .

There is inherent in the nature of life what I call "the growing edge." We see it in nature; always vitality seems to be nestling deep within the heart of a dying plant. A kind of oak tree comes to mind. You have seen it. The leaves turn yellow and die, but they stay on the tree all winter. The wind, the storm, the sleet, the snow—nothing is able to dislodge these dead leaves from the apparently dead branches. The business of the tree during the long winter is to hold on to these dead leaves. Then there begins to be a stirring deep within the heart of the tree. The expression of its life reverses itself. Its function is no longer that of holding on to the dead leaves. It turns them loose. They fall off. In their places, buds begin to come. What wind, storm, hail, sleet, ice could not do during the long winter, now comes to pass very quietly because of the vitality inherent in the tree. At winter's end people burn the dead grass, so that this growing edge, the vitality inherent in the grass roots, may manifest itself with dignity and with glory.

No expression of life exhausts life. The spirit of life broods over every living thing, just as only so long as the spirit of the hive is over the apiary can the bees live and make honey and fulfill themselves. This brooding presence is the aliveness of life.

This same principle expresses itself in human history. During the Black Death, when men were dying like flies and the masses of people were cut off from the sacraments that would have renewed their spirits and given them a sense of security in the presence of death, what happened? There came up, apparently out of the soil of Europe, a group of persons known as the Brethren of the Common Life. They said that the infinite resources of the high God were as close to each person as the beat of his heart. Even though men were cut off from the sacrament, even though there was no altar before which they were permitted to bow, the life of the living God was as close to them as their breathing. Napoleon, in the early nineteenth century, was riding high, standing like some terrifying colossus over Europe threatening to squeeze all the vitality out of every nation that did not conform to his imperious will. It was a dreadful hour! Many persons awoke each morning feeling that there was no hope for the future. Then what happened? In a log cabin in Kentucky, a baby was born—Abraham Lincoln, whose life was to set in motion a creative process that would undermine all tyrannies. And in England, another baby was born—Charles Darwin, who was to reveal to men the great plan of continuous life on earth; as if, life was saying to life, no experience, no event at any particular moment in time and space, exhausts what life is trying to do. There is always a growing edge.[15]

Notice how the text became the lens through which Thurman saw images and stories. Through his memory of the apostles after the Crucifixion he visualized an oak tree with yellow leaves in winter. The stories already within him came into focus, stories of the Brethren of the Common Life, Lincoln's and Darwin's birth at the time of Napoleon's threat. The text woven with stories propelled Thurman to lift up this prayerful affirmation of revitalization, "No expression of life exhausts life."

Howard Thurman's recall of the Brethren of the Common Life adds an important dimension to revitalization. Knowing great people is important to keeping us fresh, hopeful, and committed to ministry. We are not to limit our "friends" to those persons we can know in person. We are to cultivate the acquaintance of those of long ago and of those far away. Their stories bring them as guests to enrich us in our thoughtful, prayerful moments. In the revitalization of congregations through storytelling some in the group can be encouraged to be the raconteurs of the larger experience, the reporters of our acquaintance with the great people of faith. Pastors and well-read lay leaders can bring this gift. Also, the local church historian can, through story, help keep alive our relationship with forebears.

Stories weave together the lives of the teller and listener. Our stories weave into the biblical story. We also become part of the fabric of relations with other persons who share stories in a congregation.

The stories we hear come as gifts. We feel bound to the teller, knowing his experiences, feeling his feelings. There is the gift of deeper human relationships. Also, the gift given in the other's story often spins on to become another of our yarns. As we listen to a story, we become aware of yarns of our lives that spin out into consciousness because they are connected to the story we are hearing. The gift of stories brings us to the holy ground of religious experience. In listening to stories, sometimes we become Moses before the burning bush. We are hushed as we stand in the presence of the Holy.

Marjorie's Gift

I knew I was in the presence of the Holy when Marjorie gave me a gift and a story. Marjorie had thought about it for a long time. She then decided to celebrate her eightieth birthday by giving me a gift. She told me of her unique celebration. I protested, "Marjorie, on your birthday I'm supposed to give the gift!"

Marjorie opened before me a beautiful, antique quilt. She also unfolded a story.

"The quilt comes from Monroe County, West Virginia. As you know, that is the home county of my husband Jim's family. The quilt has been passed down through the generations and was given to me in the 1940s. It was sewn as a pastime during the Civil War as the women waited for their men to come home from the war. You are from West Virginia. You are like a son. My best gift on my birthday is giving the quilt."

At that moment I was a guest of the Holy.

As you work with groups, be aware of your priestly function. When those moments of hushed holiness come, gently call the people to prayer. The prayer may be silent or spoken by someone you ask who can comfortably pray extemporaneously. You may wish to be the one who gives words to the group's prayer.

Many of you who go through this book are leaders in your congregation who are concerned about renewing its vitality. You may have been attracted by the promise of the subtitle: "Using Stories to Transform Your Congregation." Let me offer some guidance from my own experiences of leading groups in story weaving.

One of the beauties of the method is that it can be used in solitude as well as in groups. Take some time to do story weaving on your own. You can be one who has eyes to see and ears to hear the stories because you have practiced. In solitude, discover your own biblical character. Weave one or two of your autobiographical stories into the story of your biblical character. In times alone, reflect on your good news moments: A time when you wandered aimlessly and discovered purpose, or when you were lonely and someone came to you, or when you were afraid and someone lent you courage, or when you were burdened with guilt and received forgiveness. Spin the yarn of your own personal stories from those meditations. In the silence of your own place of prayer, read scriptural texts and let them nudge to consciousness stories from church tradition, the global church, the ecumenical movement, those near to you and your personal experiences.

From these new eyes and ears for stories you may begin to cultivate the art of being a storyteller. One discipline for cultivating that art is to practice forming stories by writing them in a journal. With practice you will learn to pay attention to being specific, to using detail, to developing suspense.

One of your gifts to groups you lead is the stories you bring. You can carry stories of the church's larger experience from the Bible, Tradition, and the worldwide scene of ministry. As a storyteller, you are not just reporting information. You are linking your listeners to those in the story by letting the listeners experience what is in the story. The story engages the listeners. They participate in what happens in the story. When you tell the story of the risen Christ cooking breakfast on the lake shore, the listeners are later to be able to smell the smoke in each others' hair and clothes because they were with you sitting around the fire when Christ passed around the fish and loaves.

The art of storytelling can be worked on in private. It is no accident that you will often be renewed personally by the story weaving done in solitude.

As you use story weaving in groups, it is important you know how to invite people into the experience. The focus is not on storytelling. Do not direct groups by saying, "Tell me a story about. . . ." The lead-ins are to be open. People are pointed to areas for reflection and given the invitation and time to engage in remembering experiences. If they feel self-conscious, or manipulated or otherwise uncomfortable, they will often escape with generalizations and not specific stories. You are after stories. Later the generalizations can come as the stories are discussed. You can tell a story of your own to start things off. Remember, when people hear a story, they also hear echos of their own stories. Help them to hear their own stories!

Lead-in remarks that I find helpful are, "Recall an experience you've had or heard from someone else when. . . . Try to be as specific as possible." "Remember a time when you experienced what the people in the text experienced. Name the people, the time, the dates in your experience. Describe what happened." After the stories are told some helpful questions to use are, "What are the facts? What are the feelings? What did you learn?"

Spiritual people can be outgoing and talkative or withdrawn and quiet. Many of the most spiritual members of your congregation may be very private people. They process information inside their minds and emotions rather than think aloud. They are often careful in what they decide to talk about. They have valuable experiences and reflections to share, but can be very unsettled when put on the spot. You as leader are trying to create an environment as comfortable as the family den where people, even introverted people, feel free to share what they choose to share.

I suggest you tell your group these ground rules for sharing. First, it is all right not to share. In fact, you encourage people not to share when they feel themselves resisting. Each one has the right to decide what is private and what is offered to others. Second, times of silence will always be given. Everyone will have time to think about what he or she wants to say or not say. Silence is important for introverts, even when it is an unnecessary bother to the extroverts. Explain these rules in a low-key manner.

For the purposes of this book we are giving some detailed attention to story and story weaving. That explicit, self-conscious attention to story weaving is not to be the focus of your comments as you lead groups. Story weaving is a method. The method is to be used, but not to call attention to itself. The last thing I would recommend is a church school class called Story Weavers.

Group size is important. Primarily, conversations will occur in small groups. If you have five persons or fewer, stay in one group. With six people, divide into two groups of three. I find groups of four to be the best size. With seven or more persons in the total group, sub-groups can be formed with the basic group size as four with one or two groups with three or five persons in them. Chairs need to be movable so that persons can shift themselves from giving attention to you as leader to giving attention to each other in the small group.

Sometimes people become aware and curious about nearby groups. Laughter will erupt. A deep stillness may occur. Occasionally invite "capsule versions" of three or four stories to be told to the whole group. Some good-natured pressure and "volunteering" of others is the way the small groups decide who will retell a story to the whole group.

Timing can be awkward. Some groups will finish talking before others. A group of five will take longer than the groups of four. One way to help is let people know at the beginning of their sharing how much time they have. "Your group will have ten minutes to share experiences and reflections on the text." It helps to remind groups when they are two minutes and one minute from the end of the sharing time. You may want to speak privately with the groups of five about each one needing to share a bit more quickly. Also, be flexible, sense the moment. Sometimes ask if another minute or two is needed. You can also suggest that when someone's story has caught a listener's interest and that person wants to follow up with a question or story, he or she may mark it down to remember for break or the next time they are together. Story sharing often generates interest and action beyond the structured session. Story weaving is animating, revitalizing.

Let me offer an example of how to use the method of story weaving. Suppose you are leading a retreat of the board of your congregation. You have presented the objectives of the retreat and an overview of the schedule of activities for achieving the objectives. Fifteen people are in the retreat. You have progressed into the schedule through a get-acquainted activity during which people shared with each other in small groups. There are three groups of four persons and one group of three. Next you have participants form into a semicircle and you present a fifteen-minute lecture on the biblical concept of *Episcope*, oversight. Now you want to do story weaving to have participants know and appropriate the concept of *Episcope* on an experiential level.

Two rules are important in guiding small groups: 1. Directions must be clear and simple, 2. Directions must be given in proper sequence. Let me list the sequence. I will follow with comments that can be used in giving directions. (You will notice in the comments that some steps are repeated.)

1. **Direct people to their location for the next activity. Tell them the materials they will need.**
2. **After people are in place, briefly state the purpose of the activity.**
3. **Give instructions for doing the activity.**
4. **Designate the time allowed for the activity.**
5. **Do the activity.**
6. **Reflect on learnings from the activity.**

1. **Direct people to their location for the next activity. Tell them what materials they will need.** "For our next activity you will need to go back to your small groups. You will need to take your Bible and paper and pencil."

2. After people are in place, briefly state the purpose of the activity. "As members of the board, we have been entrusted to be overseers of the congregation. We will explore an episode of oversight in the Bible and let it help us remember experiences from our own lives. Scripture and memory will be our teachers in what it means for us to be in the ministry of oversight."

3.(A.) Give instructions for doing the activity. "Find Acts 15:1-29 in your Bible and read it silently. Read it to learn the story. As a total group, we will later reconstruct the story."

4.(A.) Designate the time allowed for the activity. "You will have ten minutes to read silently." Give people notice when only two minutes remain.

5.(A.) Do the activity. The people will read. Then you will draw them out as the total group retells the story. "What were the settings?" Antioch and Jerusalem. "What was the conflict?" Circumcision controversy, membership policy, and practice dispute. "How did they seek to resolve the conflict?" Presented the case before the apostles and elders in Jerusalem. "How was it resolved?" The inclusive membership party won, but all were given a pastoral admonition to be considerate of everyone's tradition and cultural practices. "Who was crucial in overseeing the church through this critical issue?" Apostles and elders.

3.(B.) Give instructions for doing the activity. "We are going to take some time in silence to think back and recall someone we admired or admire as an overseer of the church. In your reflections recall not only a specific person, but that person giving oversight in a specific situation. After you have relived that moment, jot down on your page the name of the 'overseer' you selected, a description of the incident, learnings that you value from that person in that situation. (Items are to be listed on newsprint.) You may also want to silently offer a prayer of thanksgiving for that person. You may even want to write the prayer and keep it with your board materials."

4.(B.) Designate the time allowed. "You will have ten minutes for silent reflection and writing. Later we will share what we would enjoy sharing with our groups."

5.(B.) Do the activity. Remember to give a warning when the time has almost lapsed.

3.(C.) Give instructions. "We have read one of the stories of oversight in the Bible. Woven into that story is the memory of someone we admire who gave oversight. Now we will weave our stories with those persons of our group. Remember my rule for sharing. You share when you listen. You don't have to speak. Tell what you would enjoy sharing. Enjoy receiving and giving."

4.(C.) Designate the time allowed. "You will have twelve minutes for everyone to share."

5.(C.) Do the activity. At the conclusion of the small group activity, you may wish to share a story of one of the overseers you appreciate. You are a storyteller. Stories come from your own life. Stories also come from the larger church. Your earlier presentation on the concept of *Episcope* would also be a good time to share stories from Tradition, the global church, and the ecumenical movement.

6. Identify learnings. "As a total group, we are going to identify our values and our learnings for our ministry of *Episcope*, oversight. Reflect aloud on learnings we can identify from Scripture and overseers we have known and overseers we have discovered in the stories we heard in our groups. As you call out values and learnings, I will list them on newsprint."

Many settings invite story weaving. First, let me discourage one setting. Story weaving is not to be publicized and organized as a great self-conscious program of congregational revitalization. Our vitality is more a matter of the Spirit than it is of good public relations. We are finding ways to tie deeply into the stories that God uses to stir the church to life. A program publicized to make the church vital is rather like the personal goal to be happy. You either are or are not, and programs to that end are mostly irrelevant. Story weaving is a method, only a method. It is to be "woven," if I may use that term, into the existing structures and programs of the church.

Three categories of settings are specifically appropriate for story weaving: the private setting, the settings of continuous-use and the settings for occasional use. In the private setting, story weaving can be used for personal prayer. It is also an excellent devotional approach to sermon preparation. The continuous-use settings are ones that do intentional Bible study. A church school class based on the lectionary is an example. Most any group in the church will benefit from occasional use. The choir can do story weaving based on the musical texts they sing. Think of the enhanced feeling that would come into the singing. An elders' retreat is an excellent place to weave stories and to be woven together into a community of leaders in mutual ministry. Other groups are the board, specially organized spiritual retreats, new member classes, the staff. The list goes on.

The congregation's departments and committees can use story weaving to help renew the church's ministry. A planning retreat at the beginning of the department's term of service is an excellent setting. Each department—worship, education, evangelism, membership, outreach, community action, property, stewardship, etc., can use selected texts from Scripture that relate to its ministry. Members of the departments can engage the text to recall stories. They weave the biblical text into their stories and into the stories that are shared by the group. Reflections on the story weaving can identify values and learnings and goals for the department.

Overworked volunteers can lead to tired congregations. Story weaving can be used to prevent burnout by helping people be clear about expectations and by offering continuing support. One way to do this is to have working groups consider their *call*, their *covenant*, the *care* they need, and the *crown* they hope to achieve. For the call, have participants weave one of their stories with Exodus 3:1-10. Then have them explore the work of the group as a call. For covenant, have them weave one of their experiences into either Genesis 29:15-30 or Ruth 1:1-18. Then have them name responsibilities, roles, and expectations for a covenant in the group. For care, have the group use Mark 9:16-29 for story weaving. Help the group name its needs for training, support, and care. The crown is the celebration of past victories and the hope of the group's future achievements. Those reflections can be woven into James 1:12-18. The congregation's valuable work can be revitalized when people perceive their work as a call that they share in covenant with others who care. They press on to the crown of celebration.

We are weavers at our first day on the job. Before us on the loom is the amazing pattern of God using stories of renewal to bring a fresh time of revitalization to the church. We see around us the hunger for authentic religious experience. We see it around us and feel it inside us. That hunger may mark a shift in the pattern being woven by our congregations. We may be moving to a *kerygma* base, a story-sharing base. Those stories can revitalize our fellowship, our learning, our mission. Prior to that we will discover how the stories must first revitalize our life of prayer and worship.

Chapter 4

Weaving Stories
That Enliven Prayer

Luke's Gospel tells a brief story of a disciple requesting Jesus to "teach us to pray." Jesus responds with a method for praying. He gives the model we call the Lord's Prayer (Luke 11:1-4).

"Lord, teach us to pray," is itself an essential prayer for congregational revitalization. Being embraced by the mystery of God brings us to life-giving religious experiences, which many in mainline congregations have been missing.

On his deathbed, church historian Wilhelm Pauck spoke of the decline of liberal churches, "They did not let the mystery shine."[16]

Parker J. Palmer asserts in his article "Borne Again" that those of us interested in the renewal of mainline congregations need to draw on the monastic tradition. ("Monk" originally included men and women contemplatives.)

Many of the books that have fed the hungers of spiritually starved Christians in recent years were written by people influenced by monasticism: Thomas Merton, Henri Nouwen, Mary Luke Tobin, and Catherine de Hueck Doherty come quickly to mind. But the essential evidence for my case goes deeper still. Monasticism is humankind's major disciplined and sustained experiment with the core concerns of today's church renewal: personal spiritual discipline, the formation of religious community, and the experience of the reality of God. . . .[17]

We need to assume God's reality if we are to create new patterns of life for ourselves and our churches. But by creating those patterns we give ourselves a chance to move beyond assumptions into experiential knowledge. It is a wonderful thing to watch people invent ways of being together and alone that rest on the faith that God will carry the burdens and hopes of their lives—and then discover, after a while, that they are in fact being borne, again and again. That discovery is the heart of monastic spirituality and the core of Christian renewal.[18]

Our hunger to be encountered by the Divine is our hope. Our hunger drives us to create new patterns of congregational life. The old pattern for most of us is one in which the foundation of the congregation was fellowship, the biblical idea of *koinonia*. It met our social needs. The new pattern is created out of our hunger for authentic religious experience. In this pattern, *kerygma*, the communicating of experiences of Good News, becomes the base. The pattern moves from hunger for religious experience to enriched experiences for prayer, to congregational life based on *kerygma*, to fellowship, learning, and mission enlivened by the *kerygma*.

"Teach us to pray." Often when that request to Jesus is stated today, a person is asking for specific methods. When I am asked for methods of prayer, I confess I am uncomfortable. I am concerned that people will confuse methods with magic. No method gives instant and constant access to a rich and exciting lifelong quest. Methods are gifts, which come as resources to be learned and tried and adapted in the continuous venture and struggle to be intentionally and consciously related to God. Methods are not magic.

Methods can be helpful gifts. I know from experience that my life of prayer has been enriched by some of the ways of prayer that have come from the monastic tradition. I will share some of those methods, but in the proper place and time. That place and time is after we explore the meaning of prayer.

Prayer is receiving. We often confuse it with giving. "I need to be more committed, and try harder to pray regularly. I need to give God his due." That little speech of self-chastisement reflects the theology of prayer as giving to God. The opposite is true. God takes the initiative and is constantly reaching for us. The primary posture of prayer is when we come with hands and hearts open to receive.

I remember the prayers of my childhood. My grandmother was not a theological scholar. Yet there was great theological insight in the terminology she chose when we prayed at mealtime. I remember her saying, "Peter, *return* thanks." You cannot return what has not been given to you. Even the thanksgiving we express to God is put in our hearts by God's initiative in seeking us and relating to us. Prayer is first receiving and then offering back to God what we have received.

Learning the ways of prayer is first learning to receive, to become guests of the Holy. Two terms may need to be defined, terms that will be used later when I describe methods of prayer. They describe ways of receiving. One is meditation. Meditation is a busy way of receiving. In meditation we block out surrounding stimuli to limit focus on a single object. Concentration is centered on a thought, image, idea, object. Our mind is often busy in imagining, recalling, and associating things with that thought, image, idea, or object.

The other term is contemplation. Meditation is active and busy. Contemplation by contrast is passive and restful. In contemplation we lay aside the work of meditation and simply are aware of the presence of God. A friend has helped me understand this elusive term by use of a metaphor. "As a little girl rests contented in the fragrance and embrace of her mother, so I rest in the fragrance and embrace of God."

How do we pray? How do we receive God? Lord, teach us to pray. To learn to pray, I suggest we stand in the presence of the saints and learn from their praying.

Mae in the Tulip Bed

One sunny morning I walked toward the building where I work and noticed Mae over in a flower bed on her knees. She was not praying. She was transplanting tulip bulbs.

Mae was one of the legendary figures around Missions Building. In the 1930s she was a missionary. She later became an executive before women were seen in leadership roles in the church. Her executive skills, her scholarship, her writing, her preaching, her lecturing, her counsel, her personal warmth were of so high a quality that she became a well-known public figure among church people in Latin America and North America. As a second career, Mae looked after the grounds around Missions Building when she retired.

I said she was on her knees transplanting tulip bulbs, she was not praying. Later I learned I was wrong. She offered a prayer for everyone who passed when she worked in her flowers. I think back now and continue to feel strength from all of those mornings, all of those greetings of "good morning," all of those prayers from Mae on her knees in the tulip bed.

To learn to pray, stand next to a saint like Mae Ward. After her death, Don, her son, edited a few of her thousands of daily letters to God. That sample of her devotional life teaches much about prayer. One small part of the lesson is Mae's method of prayer. She records it in one of her letters. I have italicized the words that outline her "rule" for prayer.

Dear God,

I am so sleepy this morning, that I could not even sing songs of praise with enthusiasm. How sweet is sleep. How rewarding is a night when the mind seems to leave the body and in some quiet, silent place enjoys peace.

Here we are, well into the new year, and here I am, well into this day. Spiritual Companions come here tonight (and I promised vegetable soup, which means a trip to the store). *The first hour and a half of each day* is well established now, God. I am slow getting started so it takes more than an hour to get dressed and have breakfast (I used to do it in less than half that time). Then I settle myself in the *Swedish chair* for a period of quiet. I begin with some relaxing and *settling-in exercises, devotional material* in both Spanish and English, with the reading and pondering of a chapter of *the Bible* suggested by one of the readings. I then *read the letters I wrote to You*, from the year before, and *write another* for the day. This gives me the chance to pray again for any I prayed for last year. Before going to bed, I read back over several years' letters. This sensitizes me to former needs and requests. I conclude the period of *"practicing the presence of God,"* by *singing a hymn* and a *few minutes of quiet*, putting the day into Your hands. In Your presence, I get up energized and, in various degrees, ready for the activities of the day.

But, my days still slip away, not at all like I want them to. I mean to get so much done in the yard at the Missions Building and I end up accomplishing so little. There are constant interruptions, though it is so hot, I wouldn't accomplish much, interruption or not. Yesterday afternoon, Mel and I went looking for trees and shrubs. I get tickled at how people think I know so much about gardening and plants. I'm always being asked questions. It goes to show that an evidence of interest and some hard work in any area tends to make one an expert! The same is true in the devotional life. I'm a learner (pilgrim is the technical term) in the strictest sense of the word, but because I am enthusiastic about prayer and have a relationship with You, and let that creep (bounce in at times) into my conversation, I am asked to speak on the subject. So I have accepted three requests to speak. See me through!

Mae[19]

We learn from Mae the importance of a set time. For her, the morning. We learn the importance of a set place, the Swedish chair. We learn the importance of a set order. Notice also the importance of memory, being aware of people and their stories.

Another method of prayer is the one I most frequently use. A little-known monk of the twelfth century by the name of Guigo II wrote a small work, *Scala Claustralium*, the Ladder of Monks. It has become for me a "ladder of prayer." This ladder of prayer I offer comes from Guigo II but is greatly shaped by my own use.

We can act on our longing for God in stages, steps, rungs that ascend, like Jacob's ladder, toward union with God. "Every round goes higher, higher." The more we search, the higher we ascend, the more the thirst for God intensifies. The ascending rungs of the ladder are reading, meditation, prayer, and contemplation.

Guigo likens the functions of the stages to the progression of taking nourishment.

Reading seeks for the sweetness of a blessed life, meditation perceives it, prayer asks for it, contemplation tastes it. Reading, as it were, puts food whole into the mouth, meditation chews it and breaks it up, prayer extracts its flavor, contemplation is the sweetness itself which gladdens and refreshes. Reading works on the outside, meditation on the pith: prayer asks for what we long for, contemplation gives us delight in the sweetness which we have found.[20]

Reading is putting the grape in the mouth. I suggest that the texts that are used come from the lectionary. The church's public worship and private prayers thus come from the same place and are connected to the lessons that are the attention of millions of Christians around the world.

The text is to be read slowly and with expectation. Awaiting in the lesson is a word from the Beloved. Read for comprehension of meanings and feelings.

Meditation is chewing the grape, the text, to extract its juices. In meditation we work with the text. Story weaving is our task. Part of the work is to use imagination to create the scene described in the text. Sometimes commentaries are useful in helping identify settings, people, issues. In meditation we bring to mind people and stories from our reading and our personal acquaintance suggested by the text. We remember moments and people from our own life. We ask, "When did I experience something similar to the experience of the people in the text or the people who first read or heard the text?"

Prayer asks for nourishment. Our intellects alone cannot attain the sweetness of knowing and feeling the presence of God for which we long.

> Lord, as I have sought you in the work of meditation, the longing and desire to know you more fully has increased. When you break for me the bread of sacred Scripture, you have shown yourself to me. The more I see you, the more I long to see you. I long no more for the outside, the crust of the letter, but the inside of the loaf in the letter's hidden meaning. Come near me, Lord God, that I may eat of the fragments that fall from the Master's table. Come near that my thirst may be refreshed by one drop of heavenly rain for I am on fire with love."[21]

In *contemplation* God comes to us in quietness and peace and we are surrounded by God's presence. We do nothing. We simply enjoy experiencing God's closeness. God understands the halting words and intentions of our prayers, and interrupts them to give the pledge of love we seek. We are sprinkled with sweet heavenly dew and anointed with most precious perfumes.

I conclude the time of prayer by "returning thanks" and "returning compassion." In meditation and contemplation many visitors come. I am aware and have present before me people whose stories have renewed my life and people whose pain has awakened compassion. God has given me these sentiments as suitable gifts to present in prayers of thanksgiving and intercession.

Many people commend the keeping of a journal of prayer experiences. I commend it on the strength of their counsel. It is not my practice.

"Lord, teach us to pray." We have stood beside two individual saints at prayer. We have been to Mae Ward's Swedish chair. We have stood beneath Guigo II's ladder of prayer. We now add our voice to a chorus that has sung continuously for twenty-eight centuries. We learn to pray as we sing the psalms.

The Psalms is the prayer book of the Bible. As we pray the psalms, we can experience a solidarity with God's people through the ages. We pray the prayers that Jesus prayed.

The psalms are the country music of the Bible. They use repetitious refrains to touch deep emotions. Country music has repetition and uses emotionally laden themes: mother, lost love, conflict, and loss. The psalms too are emotionally laden.

Some psalms evoke the emotions of integration. Others evoke the emotions of disintegration. In most every moment of our lives, we are experiencing integration, coming together; or disintegration, falling apart. Both integration and disintegration carry emotions. In times of integration we feel hope, buoyancy, anticipation, joy, celebration. In times of disintegration, we feel loss, lost, abandoned, defeated, angry, bitter, betrayed, hopeless, helpless. Those raw emotions give integrity to our praying if we learn to let the psalms touch deep emotional levels. Emotional integrity is alive in prayers that shake their fist in the face of God when we feel unjustly victimized. Emotional integrity is alive when we leave our prayer closets still whistling an ode to joy.

The psalms are an excellent way for our songs of celebration and anguish to join with those that have risen to God through the centuries. I suggest the following steps. 1. Decide the length of text. Most psalms can be prayed in one sitting. Others will need a quick preview to decide where to divide them. 2. Read the psalm slowly. 3. Name the feelings that come to mind as you reflect on the psalm. You are using your mind as a doorway to your emotions. 4. Are those feelings in tune with your feelings now? If so, what is the story? Who are the people you know or knew who felt those feelings intensely? What is their story? 5. Allow the feelings evoked by the psalm and the stories to come freely over you, both the tearful and the tuneful feelings. 6. Reread the psalm lifting up to God the words and the feelings in harmony with the saints of the centuries who have prayed the words and the feelings before you. You may wish to enter into a journal the thoughts and feelings awakened by the psalm.

"Lord, teach us to pray," is itself an essential prayer for congregational revitalization. How can we foster richer experiences of personal prayer in our congregations? One way is through spiritual direction. Persons who seek deeper experiences of prayer can be encouraged to be in a person-to-person relationship with someone mature in the ways of prayer. The focus of their discussion is always primarily on discerning the presence of God. Discussion related to healing and therapy or counseling and problem-solving may enter the conversation only secondarily as they relate to cultivating the life of prayer.

Another way to foster deeper prayer is occasionally to offer a prayer retreat for members of the congregation. During the retreat, people are given opportunities to discuss their prayer life.

They pray together in community. They pray in solitude. They are taught ways of prayer such as Mae Ward's "rule" or Guigo II's ladder or psalm praying. Those methods can be used and discussed and taken home for further adaptation.

Some members will support each other informally after the retreat. They will talk in the halls of the church or in their homes or by phone. Some will benefit from the retreat as a one-time experience. Others will need to be brought back time and again to the discipline of prayer. I suggest that the persons on retreat be called together about three or four times a year to act as a support group for each other.

Our prayers change life around us. In silence we become deeply aware of God passionately loving us and the world. The intense awareness of God's love prompts us to pray and moves us to a new orientation to life around us. We who pray are a new reality for God to use to transform the church and the world. New life is possible for us, for our congregations, even for the world.

In prayer all life is blessed. As individuals, we come from the noise and uproar and the woundings of our lives and are caressed and soothed and healed by God. The still small voice speaks and we hear it. We hear it not only in prayer but in life around us. The bush burns and we see it when we pray. Because we pray we also see it in other places.

Congregations are blessed by being places of prayer. As people come together in silence, they become open to new people, new gifts, new visions, new ways of offering ministry. Prayer as the center of life together in a congregation allows people to sense the presence of God together, to speak gently of that presence and together to let it shape their life of fellowship, nurture, worship, and service.

The world is blessed by congregations that pray. The congregation sees the world through the eyes of God. From those eyes come tears of compassion. The compassion moves the church to act with more courage to offer to the world its gifts of the gospel, justice, and shalom. In that ministry we discover our engagement with the world not only as a consequence of prayer but as the new context for meeting God. God is in the least of these, the naked, the hungry, the imprisoned, and in the most able who join us in ministry.

Spirituality is not complete as a solitary enterprise. Full prayer is finally communal. Individuals with a disciplined, intense life of prayer enrich public worship. They have perceived God in solitude, in congregational life, in the world. They have been praying the lessons in the week before they are publicly read and prayed. Because of them the hymns are more vibrant, the listening more attentive. The presence of Christ is more intensely known as the gospel is proclaimed and more intensely felt as the Table of the Lord is spread.

Chapter 5

Weaving Stories That Enliven Worship

Worship comes out of the yearning of the people of God. We and others who yearn are drawn together into a homecoming. In worship, the story that unites us is publicly spoken for us all.

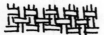 **Don't Forget the Story**

They came from Pittsburgh and Trenton and Radford, Virginia, and Lindsborg, Kansas, to say to each other, "Don't forget the story."

The need to ritualize is irrepressible. How evident that was on the summer day of the opening of the Vietnam War Memorial. The American public had said, "No memorial to Vietnam. We are guilty. We are defeated. It was a mistake. If we ignore it, maybe it will finally go away."

The monument was built. The irrepressible need to ritualize prevailed over the resistance of those who opposed the memorial. On that summer day former G.I.s from Pittsburgh, Trenton, Radford, and Lindsborg, along with thousands of others, traveled from their homes to meet by the memorial in Washington, D.C. They did not dress in fancy military regalia, but in battle fatigues. They gathered before the memorial and traced with their eyes and fingers the names of their dead buddies.

"There's Sam. I remember I had just gotten to 'Nam . . . ."

"Remember? It was a hot morning in May when Arnie got it. . . ."

They remembered. They wept. They held each other. They

sang, "God Bless America." They left saying to each other, "Don't forget the story."

Worship is remembering the story in ritual forms. It lets us remember the story by setting it in a drama with the congregation as the cast of the drama. We the cast are the new Jacob wrestling with the angel, the new Hannah praying for a son, the new people of the Exodus crossing the Jordan River and building a memorial of twelve stones, the new pilgrims singing on the way up to Jerusalem, the new followers of the Way attending the temple and breaking bread and praising God.

The whole body of the congregation relates to God in public worship. Worship is not simply individuals together in the same place at the same time for prayer. The congregation prays as church. It has a sense of its own unity as a people of God. The participation in Christ, the *koinonia*, is expanded as individuals become community and as the community's connections with the historical and worldwide Christian body are named and symbolized.

The people of God have been remembering the story through drama for a long time. I remember in the sixth century before Jesus, our people came back to Jerusalem from Exile. Most of them had never seen Jerusalem. They knew Jerusalem only from the stories of their grandparents. They came back to this unknown place to build a city, to claim home again.

Part of the claiming of home was to find some way to be molded into a people, into a community. They sought to be a people as they gathered before their priest, Ezra.

Ezra opened the Book. He read to the assembled men and women. The people responded, "Amen, Amen," lifting their hands. Moses and the law were remembered and interpreted and the community was *re*formed in that drama of retelling the story (Nehemiah 8:1-12).

That moment of Ezra opening the Word in the assembly of the people of God set in motion the service of the Word, the service of preaching. We are still remembering the story. Opening the Word before the assembly has continued by the people of God from Ezra's time up to the plans now being made for next Sunday's service of worship.

I remember one of those services when Jesus began his public ministry. In one of the literally millions of repetitions of the

75

drama of "remember the story," Jesus stood up in the synagogue in Nazareth and read Isaiah 61:1-2. "The Spirit of the Lord is upon me, because he has anointed me to preach good news to the poor; He has sent me to proclaim release to the captives and recovering of sight to the blind, to set at liberty those who are oppressed, to proclaim the acceptable year of the Lord." With the words, "Today this scripture has been fulfilled in your hearing" (Luke 4:16-21), Jesus inaugurated his ministry.

Near the conclusion of his ministry, Jesus gave us another part of the drama of remembrance. On the night he was betrayed he ate the Passover feast with his apostles. During the meal, he took a cup and a loaf and told them it was his blood and his body. As they ate, they were to "do this in remembrance of me" (Luke 22:1-38). Remember the story.

We, the people of God, have continued to remember our story in drama by recreating the scenes of Ezra reading the Word before the assembly and Jesus offering the bread and wine. We are actors in that drama. We yearn. We seek the Holy. We pray. We sing. We remember. We are joined with others at Christ's meal. We weave our ancient story retold and relived with our own personal stories and our congregation's stories.

A pastor tells two stories.

From Seeking to Celebration: Henry

"I remember Henry. I would be standing in the chancel in the early part of the service and I would see Henry's solitary figure coming in the back door of the sanctuary. He would cross the back of the church and move into an empty spot on the left side of the sanctuary, utterly alone. During the course of the service I would notice Henry's eyes look longingly at the banner hanging at the center of the chancel. He would dab away a tear from his eyes.

"You see, that banner was sewn by his wife of forty years who had recently died. During the last hymn he would slip out of the service to avoid speaking to anyone. Henry's personal grief was part of the church's total experience of bearing one another's burdens. Eighteen years ago, I remember Henry."

From Celebration to Seeking: Julia

"I remember Julia. Eighteen years ago Julia was twenty. After high school many of the young people of the youth group made their way out of church participation. Julia stayed.

"Julia's calling and longing in life was to be a mother. On that day eighteen years ago, Julia stood in the chancel to have little Bart received into the church with thanksgiving and blessing. Her individual joy was part of the church's celebration. Julia's eyes sparkled. I remember Julia."

Our people of old, and Henry and Julia, have something in common. They all come together in the church's assembly either to seek life or to celebrate life. Henry prayed, "O God, either let me die or let me live, I cannot go on in between any longer." That was what those tears were about. Julia held Bart up to the Lord and said, "Thank you, God." Our people of old gathered seeking to be a people. When they heard the Word, they celebrated by raising their hands and saying, "Amen, Amen." We seek life and celebrate it.

There is a postscript on the stories of Henry and Julia. The pastor tells it.

Henry and Julia, Continued

"It is eighteen years later and Henry is an elder statesman of the church now. He bears his part proudly. His eyes are the eyes of a person fully alive. Beside Henry now is Helen who has been there sixteen years. She continues to be the joy of his life. Henry's eyes are the eyes of one truly twice born. He comes to be part of the church's celebration of new life.

"Let me tell of Julia. Julia and Ron, her husband, have had trouble. It has been rough. Some of the early naiveté and luster is gone. Bart has been a handful. If Dennis the Menace ever lived, it was as Bart. Julia's eyes are still bright, but no longer with fluffy, romantic dreams. Julia is a survivor. She has survived because her roots go deep in the faith. Julia is still coming to be nourished by the church."

Henry started by seeking life. He now celebrates it. Julia started by celebrating life. She now comes seeking. In all of our lives there is both search and celebration as we "remember the story" and weave it into our own stories in the church's drama of Word and sacrament.

Worship is central and essential in the revitalization of congregations. Individuals are renewed and contribute to the vitality expressed in all of the congregation's life and witness. More people are affected by worship than any other activity of the church. Many equate church and worship. The action of God reaching for God's people to offer them life is often perceived in worship or not perceived at all.

Worship is the only unique action of the church. We can find all other church activities in other institutions: educating, calling to action, sensitizing to social concerns, enlisting new members, building edifices, patronizing the arts, caring for the disadvantaged, calling for gifts of money and volunteer time and talent, gathering and storing and retrieving a history. All those activities are like similar efforts in the world unless they are born out of worship. Through worship they are transformed. Who other than the church (mosque, synagogue, temple) calls people from the world to speak and touch in God's name? Worship is the coming together in response to God's initiative to dramatically retell and hear the story of God giving us life. In the effective retelling of the story lies the vitality of our faith and even the destiny of our institution.

Worship is the public event of weaving God's story into our stories. In it we celebrate God's giving of life. Liturgy is defined as the work of the people, our work. It is the work of the people involved with the work God is doing. We participate in a cosmic drama. In cosmic liturgy we look for and rehearse what God is doing. God is always reaching toward us to say, "I offer you life. Listen to all of the stories of our people yesterday and today, far and near, who have received new life."

Even in the tremendous pain and disappointments and the doubts and frustrations of this life, we do not have a world that is sick unto death. We have a world, in the language of the New Testament, that is in the birth travail of the new era. We, as the people of God, in our worship and in our work of mission, are participants with God in birthing a new era. Where do we come to realize that truth? It happens when the cosmic drama is mirrored before the assembly of the people of God in opening the Word.

Cosmic dramas are too vast for most of us to comprehend. The cosmic drama comes miniaturized for us in a simple two-act pageant. In the first act someone simply reads from the Bible. Another speaks of the reading and we respond in prayer. In the second act, the presence of Christ is known in a simple meal of bread and wine taken while listening to words that let us remember Jesus and give thanks. The life-giving themes of cosmic dimension come in a simple drama centered in a Book and climaxed in a simple, elegant meal.

How do we enhance worship as life-giving drama? I suggest three approaches: 1. A clear understanding of the actions of the drama by participants, 2. A warm inviting style of presiding by the leaders of worship, and 3. Individual story weaving by the primary cast of players in the drama, that is, by the members of the congregation.

A clear understanding of the actions of worship is important to many of us who worship in mainline churches. We are walking contradictions. We come to worship with great yearnings for a significant encounter with God. Yet we need to be in charge. Particularly our emotions frighten us. They can be so unruly, so uncontrollable. Our need to be in control of our emotions causes us to allow our emotions freedom to go only where our minds dictate. The result is that worship, which is by nature festive, becomes wooden, stodgy, and cold. We allow ourselves to invest only in the mental aspect of worship, or worse we follow the form, we *con*form, but do not engage either mentally or emotionally in worshiping.

Browbeating does not help. However, in safe, familiar settings we will allow our emotions to be caught up in the drama. Two important ingredients are 1. A familiar service that makes sense and 2. Knowledge of the intention of the actions in the service.

Familiarity frees. Novelty discourages freedom to participate fully. What a relief that the "innovative service" is now passé. The worship tradition of the early church gives us a tested and enduring pattern of worship that has beauty in its simplicity. The service of Word and sacrament offers security and familiarity. Within the set order music, visual symbols, words, shared prayers can be interesting, fresh, creative, and even innovative. When we are secure in a familiar and comfortable service, we are more apt to be mentally and emotionally responsive.

The familiar service also needs to "make sense" to many of us who need to be in control. Remember, our emotions will go where our mind allows.

The service of Word and sacrament does make sense. First comes the gathering. We as individuals assemble to be the people of God at prayer. The assembling is done briefly by the procession, a hymn, opening statements that focus our attention on God, and by a brief prayer. Our singing and praying echo the chants of pilgrims as they looked to the hills of Jerusalem while they made their way to the temple (Psalms 120-134).

Quickly the service moves to the first act of the drama. The word of God is read before the assembly as Ezra read it 2,500 years ago and as it has been read publicly ever since. The reading takes on story form in the personality and the remarks of the preacher. God has addressed us in the words of Scripture and sermon. Now we, the worshipers, are filled with the word of God. We need a way to respond. We can pour out the response in the emotional outlet of singing, or affirming our faith, or naming our concerns in the prayers of the church, or stating our commitment to a challenge that has been put before the church.

The second act of the drama brings us to our fullest response to the Word. We come to the Table of the Lord with an offering to experience Christ's presence as we respond in faith and thanksgiving. The emotions are stirred in actions of remembering Jesus, breaking bread, thanking God, eating, drinking, serving the meal to others whom we love. Even when we sit next to someone in silence, we have been together in a significant way.

Departing is done quickly. The primary acts have been completed. The cosmic drama played in miniature is over. We move expeditiously to act out our faith in the larger drama of life in the world.

That ancient model for an order of service can be used to instruct people in the sense of the service. New member classes or special elective church school courses or classes based on the lectionary are suitable places for teaching the service. Also helpful in getting the sense of the service are some brief remarks of orientation just prior to the beginning of worship, centering our attention on the themes, activities, and intentions of the service.

The congregation moves from separateness to oneness. A newcomer can feel as much a part of the service as one who has worshiped in that church for fifty years. New people are new threads woven into the pattern of the people of God at praise. When we know the sense of the service and have used an order long enough to become familiar and secure with it, we are free to be invested in the service with emotion and mind. We are free to worship in spirit and in truth.

A warm, inviting style of presiding helps revitalize worship. The presider functions as director of the drama and escort of the worshipers into the presence of the Holy.

We who preside at worship are directors of a drama. Directors of theatrical productions must know the story; must know the effect the drama is intended to create; must know how to use illusion to find deeper reality; must know how to relate to actors to bring out their gifts; must keep up with a thousand details of props, costumes, music, scenery; must have a sense of timing on when to have the drama reveal, when to hide, when to have it move, when to have it rest. We who lead, who are masters of the ceremony, are to carry those same responsibilities.

The image of the director can inform us as worship leaders. We are to know the story and how it unfolds. The story is based in a biblical text that is played out throughout the service. We are to know when the story moves, when it rests, when is the right time to reveal, when to hide. For example, we often have the prayers of intercession before the sermon. The sense of drama indicates that those prayers be after the sermon. We hold off praying until the Word has done its work of filling us with compassion. At that moment our longing to pray has intensified and God has given us a fuller prayer to offer. We know how to use illusion to find deeper reality. Symbols are our tools. Objects, sounds, metaphoric words both point to and are fused with that deeper reality. We must have a thousand details in mind. How important to have planned and prepared well as we take those first steps in the processional hymn. We bring out the gifts of the actors. That brings us to the second image for worship leaders. We are escorts.

We are privileged to escort the people of God into the presence of the Holy. Personality and the ambience of hospitality are important. We are not to call undue attention to ourselves. We are only escorts. God is host. Our sense of hospitality comes from cultivated love of both God and the people we bring before God. We approach our responsibility at lectern, pulpit, and table as worshipers with the congregation. We do not entertain or perform. We worship as we are leading others in worship. Sometimes leading means to practice the gentle art of instruction. Our instructions are cues to nudge the hearts and minds of the worshipers into the presence of God. The instructions are to be biddings that invite. An example: "In this season of Lent we become aware of Christ's suffering. Aware of his pain we feel deeply the pain of our sins. As we assemble before God we confess our unworthiness of his suffering love. Let us confess together." The art of presiding is a gentle art. We instruct but dare not become pedantic and professorial. We encourage deep investment of heart and mind. Yet, we will be totally ineffective if our encouragement is so enthusiastic it appears to be cheerleading. As escorts we are simply passing along God's invitation to come and worship while at the same time accepting that invitation ourselves.

Life-giving worship is enhanced by a clear understanding of the drama by participants and by warm, inviting escorts who direct and preside at the assembly.

Worship is enhanced by the individual story weaving of the participants. How is story weaving done in worship? People standing one after another to share stories sounds chaotic, not worshipful. Story weaving is done with preaching and in silence. Story weaving is helped by continuously teaching lectors both the skill of public reading and the skill of story weaving in private prayer.

Preaching is the obvious place for story weaving. Yarns of the Bible are spun. Yarns of the larger church are spun. Yarns of individuals are spun. All are woven into a whole fabric. But enough on preaching. A whole chapter on preaching will soon receive our attention.

Silence in worship is a time when worshipers do story weaving. Many worshipers welcome more silence. In the quiet we often become surprisingly more active in worshiping. When we participate in an arranged action, such as singing or listening to a sermon, we may or may not be emotionally and mentally engaged. When the action is self-generated, as it must be in silence, we will be engaged! When the congregation has members who have learned to do story weaving at retreats, in church school classes, in other groups, and in their private prayers through the week, they will often want the time of silence to meditate on what they have been receiving from public readings, music, common prayers, etc. The drama of worship needs both times of action and times of rest. The rest times of silence can vary from week to week. Some weeks it may come after the reading of the lessons. In other services it can move to the end of the sermon. In addition, I recommend that the usual practice be silence during the Lord's Supper. I would take away all organ background music during that time.

The training of lectors is an excellent time to teach story weaving as well as other skills that will enhance the worship of the congregation. Worship is a people drama in which the congregation is the cast of players. But the drama does not work if everyone gets up in review style to perform his or her act of worship. A parade of stars is much too busy to be worshipful. Worship as people drama is brought about by presiders, both ordained and non-ordained, who use their gifts of leadership to invite involvement and participation by everyone in the congregation. Some will be singers and musicians. In my denomination lay elders share leadership with the pastor at the Lord's Supper. An opportunity open to more people is the work of lector.

The Bible is the church's book. The preacher as one person of the church has an important stewardship of the Word, but not sole responsibility. Public proclamation of the word of God is to be done by effective reading of Scripture by non-ordained members of the church. The training of those lectors holds a special opportunity for developing clear understanding of worship, simple skills of interpreting the Bible, ability to read it effectively in public, and ways to do story weaving by using the texts of the lections as prayer resources.

I suggest that a pastor have a group of lectors in training at all times. Each group would serve for a season of the church year or part of a season. The year starts with Advent. During October and November, the pastor meets the team for Advent to train them. That group would help lead the services of Advent, Christmas, and Epiphany. The next team would lead the services in the ordinary time between Epiphany and Ash Wednesday. Other teams would lead from Ash Wednesday through Holy Week, the Easter season through Pentecost, the first half of ordinary time, and the second half of ordinary time.

Each group would meet two or three times prior to the beginning of its season. In the first session the group would study the history and character of the seasons of the church year with special emphasis on the one the group will help lead.

The act of God offering new life is incarnate principally in the life story of Jesus Christ. Each year the church relives that life and life-giving story in two great cycles of seasons. In the Passion and in Easter the church's proclamation is rooted in Christ's death and resurrection. In Christmas and Epiphany the church's proclamation is rooted in the manifestation of God among us as the one born Jesus of Nazareth. In both of the cycles there is a time of preparation: Advent for Christmas, Epiphany; Lent for Passion and Easter. The Easter season is concluded with the Holy Spirit's coming to create the church at Pentecost. The two great cycles are times when the church's festivities rise above ordinary time. In ordinary time the people of the church acknowledge the ordinary, day-to-day business of ministry, of living fully into their baptisms.*

The lectors would also study the actions and intentions of worship in the order of service. Information in this chapter and in other resources can be used.† At the conclusion of the first session, lectors are assigned to the Sunday they will serve.

In the second session the group would open the Scripture, their special trust in the ministry of worship. The lectionary can be explained. Simple questions for interpreting the Bible will be introduced, as well as resources for answering those questions.

God addresses the church through the Bible. The lectionary is a tool that systematically proclaims the Word to the church. Three lessons from the Bible are selected for reading each Sunday. Most often there is a lesson from the Old Testament, from an epistle of the New Testament, and from one of the gospels. In the case of the Easter cycle and Christmas cycle, the lessons are selected to proclaim the season being celebrated. In ordinary time more attention is given to continuous readings of selections that are representative of the total biblical narrative. The readings

---

*Recommended resources: 1. *A Pilgrim People* by John H. Westerhoff, III, available from the Seabury Press; 2. *Seasons of the Gospel* by James F. White, available from Abingdon.

†Recommended resource: *Thankful Praise* by Keith Watkins, et al., available from CBP Press.

continue for three years and then begin again. Each year features one of the Synoptic Gospels: Year A, Matthew; Year B, Mark; Year C, Luke.

If God addresses the church through the Bible, then the leader does not rightly ask, "What will I preach about next Sunday?" Or, "What will the themes of worship be next week?" Or, "What do the people want or need now?" Those questions lead to distorted portions of Scripture being proclaimed. They also prejudge what the word of God will say in a given situation. The hearer becomes the source rather than the recipient of the proclamation. With the lectionary, the readings are selected to be representative; the leader does not come to the text with a need or theme in mind but with openness to let the service be formed from prayerful meditation on the Word. In addition, the lectionary helps give the congregation solidarity with millions of other Christians who will hear and pray the same lessons at the same time.*

The lectors in training will be helped to understand their texts by the introductory questions of biblical interpretation. Use a sample text and have them do a first reading. Then they are to write a paraphrase. The Bible contains a variety of literature. Some of our ancient people sang the story. Others recited it in affirmations in public worship. The story was told in riddles and parables and in pastoral counsel in letters. Ask the lectors to identify the type of literature they are reading. Is it parable, song, creed, admonition, law, etc.? Next, they are to discover who were the first readers. What issues in the lives of the readers were being addressed? Who wrote to them? What was said regarding their situation? What are the key words? Next have the lectors look into the commentaries to discover their answers. They conclude the exercise by rewriting the paraphrase.

Lead them now into story weaving. Using the "ladder of prayer" described in Chapter 4, help them use the lesson to pray. In climbing the ladder of prayer, they see the stories around them in their own lives as continuations of God's story. Suggest that

---

*Recommended resources: 1. *The Common Lectionary* by ICEL, available from The Church Hymnal Corporation, 800 Second Avenue, New York, NY 10017; 2. *The Word in Worship* by William Skudlarek, available from Abingdon.

they use the lessons of the next few Sundays as a resource for their own private prayer.

Some training is to be offered in public reading. The lectors are not to weave a story as a part of the lesson. That is the work of the preacher and the listeners. They may make a one- or two-sentence statement of context or description to help the listeners. The lectors "set the warp" on the loom. By clear reading the lectors will help the listeners do their work of story weaving as they listen or as they meditate in times of silence during or after the service. The lectors will do the important work of proclamation in their preparation and public reading of the lessons. The gift of their leadership will set Scripture before the congregation as the common story shared by the people of God.

The lectors then practice by going to the lectern and reading aloud. The pastor may wish to have a speech teacher come in for the first few groups. By observing the teacher's coaching the lectors, soon the pastor will learn how to gently critique future lectors.

By having teams of trained lectors, a congregation will enhance its worship. A significant and growing number will come to all future services with a clearer understanding of the story retold through drama. They will know what is happening and be able to be involved in worship not only by following the outward form of the service but by being engaged mentally and emotionally in the intentions of the action. The Bible will be used as a book of private prayer as well as common prayer. It will be a book of all the people of the church, not just the clergy. Lectors and former lectors will be able to make good devotional use of the silence to do story weaving, the knitting of their lives into the great story of cosmic dimensions, the story of God offering life.

An audience seated in a theater before the curtain opens is aware of distance, barriers, and separation from the stage. When the play begins and the drama works, the distance, separation, and barriers dissolve. The world at that moment is a stage with the audience participating by riveted attention, rising feelings, tears, and laughter.

The congregation's irrepressible need to ritualize its hopes and fears brings it again and again to worship. We of that congregation come as skeptics. "I dare you, show me that life has meaning." "Show me that high values and commitment are worth the pain and sacrifice." "Show me that I can be encountered by the Divine and life can be fresh with joy and hope and new energy and resolve." We come with our skepticism yet with a deep, often hurting, hope that something will break through our skepticism. "Please, please, show me."

We come not just as isolated individuals wanting to be near God. We come to be a part of other seekers. In common quest we come into each other's presence as well as God's presence. We come to be woven into a community at prayer daring to ask, "Please, please show us that life has meaning."

Unfolded before us is an ancient drama of an old priest reading an ancient book before a new group of settlers. A table is spread before us with simple dishes and food, a chalice and paten, bread and wine. But when it is done well, sometimes the distance, the barriers, and the separations dissolve and we are the players on a heavenly stage. Our stories fit with The Story. Our hearts are strangely warmed. Our prayers of, "Please, please, show me" are answered. We come back from the drama knowing that we have been guests of God and life is new.

Chapter 6

Weaving Stories
That Enliven Preaching

People today in mainline congregations openly express their longing to experience the presence of God in church. A shift may be occurring in congregational life that makes *kerygma*, proclaiming or sharing the gospel, the dominant value in church life. This chapter is to help those of us who preach to make full use of this new opportunity. If you do not preach, you are still invited to read on, to listen in on this dialogue between preachers.

I invite preachers to dialogue with me. One of the beauties of preaching is its distinctive individuality. It is an art form. The art piece is conceived and put into form by an individual and carries the distinctive marks of that individual. I will risk speaking of that art form that carries the fingerprints of the soul. I do not presume to tell anyone how to preach. But I do intend to open the subject of storytelling in the art of vital preaching. The art of preaching is cultivated by practice and reflection on the practice, I invite preachers to a time of reflection.

Preaching is significant for revitalizing congregations. Preaching as story weaving is a golden thread that is woven into the fabric of congregational renewal.

The golden thread, the stories in the sermon, is visible, valuable, and "vitalizing." Visible: The rich-looking golden threads of a garment catch the eye. Preaching is the most public form of story weaving. Valuable: Sermons engage listeners and usher them into the presence of the Divine. The religious experiences generated by effective preaching can be transforming to worshipers and congregations. "Vitalizing": Pulpit stories, well woven from Scripture, Tradition, and contemporary life cause worshipers to remember and be renewed by their own stories, their own experiences of good news.

Stories make sermons visible, valuable, and "vitalizing." Consider the contrasting promise and lack of promise in two introductions to Epiphany sermons.

Misfit at the Manger

Six-year-old Eric, having turned his bathrobe inside out so "Dallas Cowboys" doesn't show, takes his place in the procession of magi and begins his slightly off-key rendition of "We Three Kings." The glint in his mischievous eyes causes us to look for other clues that he is a miscast wiseman. Under that gold spray-painted cardboard crown lies blond hair that defies any comb to conform it to any semblance of neatness. That Dallas Cowboys robe covers jeans in whose pockets are one quarter for the video arcade, one string saved for tying the neighbor's cat to the swingset, and one "He Man" ring that glows in the dark. Under the slightly frayed elbow of that robe is a large Band-aid covering an injury received when trying to climb the Christmas tree. Our king also has a smudged cheek, evidence of a mother's game effort to make Eric more kingly with saliva and handkerchief briskly applied.

Our little king seems a misfit at the manger.

How suitable Eric is to the Gospel of Matthew's story of wisemen and star and stable and kingly gifts. Matthew's is the story of the aliens, strangers, misfits, the "others." It is the story of aliens in adoration.

The second introduction points to a sermon that will begin, continue, and end on an abstract level.

> Epiphany is a season based in the concept of God manifested among us. We will explore the meaning of that concept and its value for our lives.

The "Eric" introduction is not even fully a story. "Eric" is a Norman Rockwell-styled painting created with words. Like a Rockwell painting it suggests a story; it touches the memory and experience of the listeners and invites them to create the story. This Epiphany introduction promises a sermon in which people can later talk about unexpected persons they have met who helped them discover who is the real king. By contrast, the sermon introduced with "Epiphany is a season based in the concept" promises at best a response of "that was an interesting idea."

Stories surprise us. They are so specific that we assume that they will exclude people. If you tell a story of a towheaded little boy with his dog, what happens if you were never a little white boy with a dog? What if you grew up black, female, and had a cat? Surprisingly, the specificity of stories does not exclude. The specific has power to speak universally as listeners empathize with the characters who reflect their experience through the story. By contrast, the all-inclusive, no-edged abstraction floats by like a cloud. Stories give sermons visibility. They enhance their value. They are "vitalizing."

Visible, valuable, "vitalizing" are not descriptions often associated with preaching today. The common complaint is that preaching is dull or that it is an harangue. Because of dullness, worshipers do not stay attentive to the preaching despite their resolve to do so. In sermons that harangue, worshipers do not experience hope or love. The gospel is missing in sermons that rarely venture beyond admonitions. Consider this summary of American preaching given a few years ago. The message of American preaching is please, for God's sake, try harder to be good. Sadly, this preaching has been effective. In a 1983 survey 41 percent of the people polled agreed with the statement, "The gospel is God's rules for right living."

I offer skilled story weaving as an alternative to sermons that are abstractions floating above the reach of the congregation. I offer skilled story weaving as an alternative to "Please, for God's sake, try harder to be good." Story weaving is the essence of preaching for revitalization. Ronald Allen who teaches preaching at Christian Theological Seminary defines preaching as, "The interweaving of the gospel story and the contemporary story in such a way that the contemporary is shaped by the gospel story."[21]

Please note that our discussion is on *skilled* story weaving. I am not simply urging those of us who preach to pep up our sermons with more stories. Stories hold attention. We who speak are often tempted to use them as a rhetorical device simply because we know they work in keeping the interest of an audience. The unconsidered use of stories as a public speaking device can produce sad and disastrous results. One preacher told the story of his unfaithfulness to his wife. He had no trouble keeping his audience's attention that Sunday. But the effect was embarrassment and disillusionment. No gospel was in that story of public confession nor later in the preacher's ruined marriage and dismissal from the church.

In another church the congregation sat in rapt attention as a prospective pastor strung story after story in an introductory sermon. Later the pulpit committee met and discussed the prospective pastor's visit. They concluded that the "talk" was entertaining but they were not sure it was preaching. A teenager on the committee asked, "What will he say three months from now when he runs out of stories?" The pastor wasn't called. Story weaving is an art that goes beyond collecting and telling stories. Preaching is interweaving the gospel story and the contemporary story in such a way that the contemporary is shaped by the gospel story. But how do we do it?

I do not presume to have the definitive answer. I offer my reflection and learning as a way to stimulate your reflection and learning. Some of what I offer is original. Most comes from my teachers of preaching, originally Dwight E. Stevenson and Richard C. White; recently Fred B. Craddock. The learning has been integrated so that I have lost track of what insights and skills come from which source.

How do you develop the skill of story weaving in preaching? Let me offer my answer to the question to prod you to think about your answer. 1. Be in the presence of great preaching, 2. Plan ahead, 3. Follow faithfully the vocational "rule" of four phases of preaching. Let me expand.

Be in the presence of great preaching. Perry Gresham, Warren Hastings, James Hempstead, Lester McAllister, L.N.D. Wells: After almost forty years I can still name them. These are the preachers who came as distinguished guests to the pulpit of our church when I was a child and young teenager. The congregation planned for months ahead. Eagerness intensified as the week of preaching approached. Friends came from other churches in town. We were stirred by these gifted preachers. I believe in the great impact of preaching. I'm like the old joke of one Baptist testing the orthodoxy of another. "Do you believe in sprinkling?" asked the inquisitor. "Believe in it!" came the response, "I even saw it once!"

Do I believe in great preaching? I even saw it once! For my own preaching to stay vital I need to hear great preaching from time to time. Sermon subscriptions from a favorite preacher, cassettes, assemblies, and seminars all help. When I hear preaching that lures me into the presence of God, I leave as a transformed preacher. My fresh belief in the power of preaching gives my own efforts a new burst of energy.

One of the advantages today over my childhood is the opportunity to hear more women who are emerging as gifted people in the pulpit. I also make a point as a white person to hear black preachers. Their passion often blows on the low-burning embers of my preaching and I am brought to fuller flame.

Listen to great preachers. Allow their sermons to work on you. Later note their use of stories. You will discover your own master teachers.

Plan ahead. One way to plan ahead is to make regular retreats. You take a Bible and lectionary and get away from phones and meetings. An advantage of the lectionary is that it saves the random searching for a text, or worse, a topic. Even with the lectionary you still need to plan ahead. Every three months, make a day-long retreat to read through the lections for the approaching three months. Into thirteen files put 1. The list of lections for the Sunday, 2. A star beside the lection chosen for preaching, 3. An indication of the parameters of the text (you may decide to make the text longer or shorter than the lectionary), 4. Any preliminary thoughts on the text. As you approach the time of preaching, you may find material to drop into the active preaching files. You also help the musicians of the church and the leaders of church school classes, which may be based on the lectionary, by giving them your text ahead of time. They too need creative brooding time.

Follow faithfully the vocational "rule" of four phases of preaching. We come now to the heart of our calling, our vocation, as ministers of Word and sacrament. We in religious vocation are called to serve God. Our ministry is to bring us into a deep relationship with God. Our vocation is the cultivation of that relationship. Our vocation has an active dimension, it also has a prayerful, contemplative dimension. In the monastic traditions the active and passive dimensions are pursued in a "rule" or discipline that alternates work and prayer.

Our preaching is really a public witness to the gospel that emerges out of our active and passive cultivation of our relationship with God. Preaching is an extension of prayer. Preaching brings together work and prayer so that the preacher may be an able instrument for the proclamation of the gospel. We who would preach well need the full and faithful discipline of a "rule." I offer my "rule" of four phases for preparing for preaching: 1. Preparing the preacher, 2. Discovering the message, 3. Creating the sermon, and 4. Preparing the preaching. I will describe what happens in each phase. The description will become quite specific as I show how stories were developed in one of my sermons as it went through the four phases of preparation. (The entire sermon is printed as Appendix B.)

First, for effective preaching, the preacher, not the sermon, must be prepared. In this phase the preacher is the lover. He or she opens the Bible to the lection for the sermon like a lover opens a letter from the beloved. The preacher becomes prepared by using the text for expectant reading, meditation, and contemplation as he or she climbs toward God on a ladder of prayer.

You may wish to review the ladder of prayer as it was described in Chapter 4. Remember the rungs: Read the text expectantly, meditate on the text, pray, be aware of the presence of God in contemplation. This is the time for naive reading of the text. Without thought of commentaries or the issues of criticism, approach the text in holy innocence, for now asking only "What is God saying to us in this lesson?" Climb the next rung of the ladder toward God by meditating on the text. "Whom do I know who is experiencing the situation or the message of the text? Have I had that experience? What are the images and stories that connect my life to the text?" After meditation climb to the rung of prayer expressing to God the intense longing to be near God. Move then to restful receiving and complete openness to God's presence.

I opened the Gospel of Luke in preparation for the third Sunday of Easter. I found the text and read:

Then they told what had happened on the road, and how he was known to them in the breaking of the bread. As they were saying this, Jesus himself stood among them. But they were startled and frightened, and supposed that they saw a spirit. And he said to them, "Why are you troubled, and why do questionings rise in your hearts? See my hands and my feet, that it is I myself; handle me, and see; for a spirit has not flesh and bones as you see that I have." And while they still disbelieved for joy, and wondered, he said to them, "Have you anything here to eat?" They gave him a piece of broiled fish, and he took it and ate before them.

Then he said to them, "These are my words which I spoke to you, while I was still with you, that everything written about me in the law of Moses and the prophets and the psalms must be fulfilled." Then he opened their minds to understand the scriptures, and said to them, "Thus it is written, that the Christ should suffer and on the third day rise from the dead, and that repentance and forgiveness of sins should be preached in his name to all nations, beginning from Jerusalem. You are witnesses of these things" (Luke 24:35-48).

I let my imagination reconstruct the scene of the disciples in grief. I felt as best I could what they felt. In meditation I went back to a funeral scene that occurred when I was five years old. I still remembered the somberness and sadness as I looked at the amber floor lamps that stood by my grandfather's casket. A pastor friend also came to mind. He had been so hopeful on accepting his call to the church. Now he is leaving discouraged and defeated. In contemplation, friends came to me who had recently experienced death. I prayed for them. Also a small fragment of a memory came back. I recalled a man, I do not remember who, telling me of going to his wife's grave to talk alone (Or was he alone?) about the woman he now wanted to marry. He visited his wife's grave often but this was the first time he left humming a happy tune.

In my meditation I also remembered a special time with Loren. Later the congregation would hear that story as I wove it into the biblical story.

A Touchable Jesus

A young pastor came to that moment of his first conflict with his first congregation. The subject of the conflict was so small that it has now faded past the point of recall. But when he was twenty-seven years old the subject must not have seemed small for he still can remember the feelings of being afraid and lost. He called his regional minister and talked by phone. A couple of days later the phone rang and it was the regional minister. He said, "I'm in town to take you to lunch." The young minister never knew if he drove over just for him or if he was passing through. He doesn't remember what was said at lunch, but does remember the feelings. He was in the presence of a good, strong man of faith. He absorbed perspective on the problem, strength and faith. He needed a touchable Jesus—and at that moment his pastor became his touchable Jesus. That regional minister was Loren

Lair of Iowa. I was the young minister. In my memory now is a picture: a table with the plates of a finished lunch—cups with the last drops of coffee in the bottom—plates with olive pits on the side. I remember another deeper picture of a table and plates with fish bones on the side—and a chalice with a little leftover wine. "He was known to them in the breaking of bread."

Second, for effective preaching, the preacher must do the work of discovering the message in the text: the lover of phase one becomes for a while the scholar of phase two. Learned colleagues are to be assembled to engage you in dialogue about the text. These scholarly friends come to you in the commentaries and resource books on the Bible. I stay with the simple exegetical questions. Who were the first readers/hearers? What are they experiencing that is being addressed by the author? What is being said to those first readers? What kind of literature is it? What is the text's context in the book? Do any literary threads connect it with other passages in the book? The Bible? What are the significant words? Where in the text does the action shift?

All of those questions will receive attention. But, the sequence of asking is important in preaching that uses story weaving. Questions about people are asked first. Story preaching is specific and person centered. The first questions to ask the panel of scholars on the pages you open are who were the characters in the text and who were the people being addressed by the writer? What were they experiencing? How did the writing likely affect their lives? The other questions are helpful and interesting background that fill in more information about people being encountered with the word of God.

Among other discoveries I learned that the people who first read Luke were in the turmoil of the docetic heresy. Was God really in this earthly Jesus who died? Jesus may have been an hallucination. I learned that this text describes a pivot point from the disciples' grief to their life-giving ministry as told in Acts. My learned colleagues also showed me that Luke repeatedly indicated the value of knowledge in bringing his readers to salvation. He also left a trail of dirty dishes through his writings. Significant moments of revelation were presented in settings with meals.

At this point, I thanked the scholars for their very able assistance and dismissed them. I carefully and slowly reread the text with my new learning in mind. I became lover/scholar as I took my meditation further to remember moments when I was given new life by someone coming in person. I recalled Loren again. I remembered meeting De Vee. I came up with the term "touchable Jesus." After three false starts I wrote in one sentence the message the text had given me. "In times of deep pain in our lives, God's healing comes from specific, tangible people who send us on to be specific, tangible healers for others." My message was finished, but the sermon had not started.

The most common fault I find with sermons given by committed, conscientious preachers is what I call phase two sermons. The pastor works hard in sermon preparation, but he becomes so intrigued by the scholarship that he (this is rarely a fault in the women's sermons I hear) loses charge of the sermon. Instead of using scholars as helpful colleagues, he lets them take over the sermon. The work and prayer of phases three and four are not done. The message is discovered but the sermon is never created nor the preaching prepared.

After discovering the message it is time for a long break before beginning to create the sermon. In this break between phases two and three let me tell you the story that came to me as I meditated in phase two.

Meeting De Vee

It was an experience veiled in mystery. De Vee was a friend from Iowa who had moved to Cleveland. I had a stopover in the Cleveland airport one day and decided to call my old friend. No answer. The public address speaker announced that the flight to Chicago and Cedar Rapids was delayed. I walked over to Gate Twelve on the remote chance I would know someone going to Cedar Rapids. There sat De Vee bathed in amber light, quietly weeping. I went to her. We touched and talked. Later in the lunchroom I heard the reason for the tears. A daughter-in-law had forbidden contact between this mother and her son and grandchildren. As she finished her story, she reached over and touched my hand and said, "God sent you to me today." She needed a touchable Jesus that moment and I, filled with wonder, had been sent. I looked at the table in the airport restaurant and saw a bit of broken bread and I remembered another deeper picture of a table and plates and fish bones on the side and a chalice with a little leftover wine. "He was known to them in the breaking of bread."

Phase three of sermon preparation is creating the sermon. Up until now the preacher has engaged the text as lover and as scholar. The preacher now becomes artist.

Our objective as artists is to move the sermon from message, that is concept, to experience. Using words, we seek to paint pictures in which the congregation experiences feelings and thoughts similar to those of the persons in the text and/or the feelings and thoughts of the first readers and hearers of the text. Stories and images are the "stuff" of our art. They are our paint, our marble, our musical notes, our yarn. We weave the stories not to help people "get the point" nor to keep our audience's attention. Stories artfully woven in preaching are an art form that recreates experiences.

My work as artist begins as I center myself with a few moment's silence and prayer. In that centering time I reread the text. I gather around me the memories from when I was praying the text as a lover and when I was digging into the text as a scholar. I next read my wording of the message, my last work as a scholar. My message from Luke 24:35-48: "In times of deep pain in our lives, God's healing comes to us from specific, tangible people who send us on to be specific, tangible healers for others."

How do I attempt to transform that concept into an art form for people to experience? The first step is to determine the movement of the biblical text, and divide the text into a pattern of scenes that will form the overall fabric of the sermon. The movement and scenes from Luke 24:35-48 came out for me as, 1. Persons desolate from pain and loss (v. 33), 2. are encountered by a touchable Jesus (vs. 36-44), 3. who sends them on to be wounded healers to others (v. 46 and on through Luke and Acts).

My next work as artist is to put the warp into place. Looking at the design I have created from the text I decide when and how to tell the story from the Bible. Here is the story of part of the Luke text that was written to help worshipers know the disciples as "persons desolate from pain and loss."

An Amber Room

"The eleven gathered together and those who were with them" (v. 33). In ten scant words Luke sketches the background. We fill in the details, paint in the colors. Ten scant words: "The eleven gathered together and those who were with them."

The scene is familiar to all of us, especially pastors who have been in dozens of living rooms with families after a funeral. Here is a drawing together, a huddling in common hurt. Yet each one is strangely alone with his or her own regrets, doubts, guilt, aching loss.

Luke invites us into a very deep, private moment in the life of the disciples. Amber walls have been sooted by oil lamps. The varying tones of the amber walls are dimly lit now by those lamps. The light also illumines the amber skin of sad Palestinian faces.

Here in a corner a small group talks quietly of sunny days in Galilee and Jesus' words, "Come follow me." Unsaid is the thought, "Would I have followed if I had known it would hurt so much now?"

There one of them sits alone and remembers the beautiful experience on the mountain of transfiguration. It was about then that everything started to change. Jesus started talking of being delivered into the hands of men. They began making their way to Jerusalem. Maybe that was the point when they went wrong (9:28f, 44, 51).

Into the silence of the amber room another ventures the words "and they crucified him." The unspoken reply in all their hearts was, "Could I have prevented it . . . what did I do wrong?"

The group is leaderless, lifeless, lost.

As artist I now select and create the woof to be woven into the warp. The stories come from reading, plays, stories told by others, the larger church, experiences of friends, events in my own life. The latter two, of course, must be used with discretion. By this time in sermon preparation I rarely have trouble finding stories. We all have more stories than we realize. In meditation, prayer, and study of the text, we are given eyes to see and ears to hear the stories of the gospel in life around us and in our own lives. For many sermons the painful part of the work as artist is deciding the stories to eliminate.

After selecting and creating the stories of the woof, I begin writing the sermon. (How envious I am of those of you who don't have to put your sermons into manuscript form.) In the writing I am weaving the warp of the Bible story with the woof of our story with the artistic objective of engaging the congregation in the experience of the story. In the sermon I have chosen for an example, I do not talk about pain and desolation but I seek through story weaving to help people be in touch with the pain and desolation they have known. In the second scene in the design, I do not talk about the heresy of docetism but through stories seek to bring the worshiper into the presence of Christ in the tangible people who have loved them in their own lives. This is the Good News in the sermon. The third scene of the design is not an admonition to do better. In the experience of their own wholeness the worshipers are beckoned into the mystery of God that works through their lives to touch others.

The story of Loren, "Touchable Jesus," came from my first meditation on the text. In the time of naive reading and meditation as lover, I remembered Loren coming to me to give me strength and hope. Stories of the woof of the sermon for me most frequently come from the first phase of preparation. Many other stories also come then, which my work as scholar causes me to eliminate as not having integrity with the text. Others are eliminated because they are too personal or call too much attention to myself or someone known by the congregation. Loren's story was simply put into the sermon without modification. In this case the story is a factual report.

The story "Meeting De Vee" came to me in a time of meditation in phase two, or the scholarly phase. Note that the divisions are not pure. The scholar is primarily scholar but also lover in phase two. In phase three the preacher is principally artist but also lover and scholar. To weave De Vee's story into the sermon I took some artistic license. I wanted to keep Luke's continual use of meal scenes as events of revelation. I created the setting of the airport restaurant at the end of the story to bring in Luke's food motif.

The story of George in "Cupcakes and Grace" was created entirely for the sermon. The inspiration for the story came from a tiny fragment of memory that came to me in meditation in phase one. The story was intentionally created in phase three as artist. To see how the stories all weave into the warp of the Bible story I suggest you read Appendix B.

Cupcakes and Grace

George had not driven by the cemetery near his home for two years without shedding a tear, or sighing, or experiencing an unexpressed inner ache. George's Sara died two years ago. Two years, and George still wasn't back to living. He tried playing golf again, but to please the friends who worried about him, not for the enjoyment. He went to work. But work was putting in time. No exhilaration came from the challenges, no satisfactions from the accomplishments.

George's route to work, to church, to the shops went right by the cemetery where Sara was buried. For two years George drove by that cemetery every day and he had yet to drive by without a tear, a sigh, or an unexpressed inner ache.

Something extraordinary happened to George. George got acquainted with Roberta. He awakened to her wit and her touch. But Roberta, surprisingly, compounded the problem.

There were still the drives by the cemetery. Now George was deeply troubled by feeling guilty that he may replace Sara with someone else. He felt disloyal to forty years of marriage and to Sara's memory. He felt he was unfaithful to the grief that had become deeply bonded to him in two years. George began to spend agonizing hours by Sara's grave. George would weep with joy when with Roberta, then would weep with guilt by Sara's grave.

One day a wise friend dropped by who had been through a similar experience. George was a little flustered. Sara was the one who knew what to do when company dropped in. But George managed to put on a pot of coffee and got a couple of Hostess cupcakes out of the freezer. Over the coffee cups and cupcake wrappers the friend reached out and took George's hand and said, "You know, George, it is because of Sara's love of forty years that you need and can fully give love to Roberta. It's OK to love and be loved." The friend for a moment became a touchable Jesus. "He was known in the breaking of bread." George accepted the words but did not think about them until the next day. The words and his friend's touch came back as he drove past the cemetery and caught himself whistling. No tear—no sigh—no unexpressed inner ache. Life had begun again!

Phase four moves us to preparing for preaching. After being a lover at prayer, a scholar at research and reflection, an artist at creating illusions that reveal truth through the reliving of experiences, the preacher moves to the final phase in preparation for being an effective communicator, a proclaimer of the gospel.

My own last work of preparing for the moment of standing in the pulpit has me working on delivery. In the day and a half before preaching I go through the sermon five times. The first time I read it through aloud, hearing my own voice saying the words, familiarizing myself with the material, doing minor polishing of the writing. The next time I read, again aloud, with a consciousness of timing. This time through I put in pause marks and note phrases to repeat. The third time through I take a walk without the manuscript. I talk through the sermon. This time I often imagine a specific person, preferably one in the congregation. At the beginning of each scene I discipline myself to tell my friend in a simple sentence what that scene is to communicate or to do. Within three hours of the service I read the sermon two more times aloud. I also try to take two minutes to stand in the pulpit to make sure I can see my manuscript, to look over the pews and imagine people in them, and to say the opening words of the sermon.

I suspect that I need more work in phase four than most preachers. I also suspect that many preachers need more phase four work than they realize. Preparing the preaching, the delivery, helps the sermon reach out and connect to the listener. At its best it completes the preparation for the moment when the gospel story interweaves with the worshipers' stories in such a way that worshiper and congregation are transformed.

Stories have power. They can be misused and robbed of their power or, worse, misused to distort the gospel. Three guidelines can help prevent the misuse of stories.

The first guideline is never to use stories that call attention to ourselves or individuals personally known to the church. Our stories of the pastor as hero detract attention from the gospel. Worshipers are offended at what appears to be bragging. When we tell a story of the pastor as victim, we will also likely draw away from the gospel. The compassion of the congregation will be directed toward us. That is not the purpose of preaching the gospel.

Autobiographical stories are to be limited. (In the sermon example in this chapter a weakness is the use of two autobiographical stories.) We are also to use only those autobiographical stories in which we are incidental characters. Additional personal stories can be used if we are well disguised. We become stories of "a friend" or "a pastor I know." Cute stories about our children or grandchildren are to be closely measured. Some humanizing self-disclosure can be helpful in communicating the gospel. However, it can quickly become excessive and inappropriate. When our self-disclosure calls attention to ourselves, we detract from the very message we wish to proclaim.

More risky than the autobiographical stories are those of persons well known to the congregation. People are embarrassed and put on the spot. Attention is taken from creating illusions that help the whole congregation experience the gospel when they are responding with "Jim is a great guy" or "Poor Mary." I do not even risk using stories of parishioners by disguising them with changed names and settings.

The second guideline is never to use a story within the first month you hear it. The powerful story to a public speaker is like steak before a hungry dog. We who speak have a hard time resisting. What happens is that we become so eager to use a "hot" story that we let it distort the text. We "shoehorn" the story into the sermon and the story weaving loses integrity. The text is the warp, not the latest hot story we bring back from a church assembly.

The third caveat is not to preach character sermons. By character sermons I mean the preacher assumes the identity of a character and plays that character, speaking his or her lines in first person throughout the sermon. Most of us cannot resist this temptation at least once. If you insist on character sermons, do one and get it out of your system. Your congregation wants you to be you. Assume character parts only for a sentence or two where it is obvious you are simply dramatically quoting the character.

Preachers often ask me where I get stories and how I remember them. The answers are no mystery. Like a reporter with a notebook I see potential stories in everything I do and take notes. Stories come from reading, movies, television, other preachers, conversations. Those stories I jot down and drop in a file.

Primarily, however, stories are remembered experiences discovered during times of praying using the sermon text. The text becomes the lens through which we receive the clarity of the gospel experienced in life around us and beyond us and within us. Meditating on the text gives us eyes and ears to see and hear the stories.

Imagination is another source of stories. I find nothing ethically compromised in creating stories to communicate truth. "Cupcakes and Grace" was created in the sermon I am using as an example. In fact, sometimes in phase three of preparing for preaching we can come to a spot that we know needs a story and nothing from our meditations on the text comes to mind. We cannot remember a story from our reading. No more exciting time exists in sermon preparation than when we turn our imagination loose and create a story.

Imagination enhances preaching. The created story comes from imagination. Imagery comes from imagination. Details and highlights from imagination enhance the telling of stories from reading or remembered experiences or from other storytellers.

John Brown's One-Legged Parrot

Fred Craddock, one of America's outstanding preachers, tells of the gift of imagination received from his father.

When the Craddock children came home from school, they would often be met by their father.

"What did you study in school today, children?"

"Oh, not much, but we did learn about John Brown, the abolitionist from Kansas."

"John Brown . . . John Brown. It's a little-known fact so maybe your teacher didn't tell you this. Did you know that John Brown, the abolitionist from Kansas, once had a one-legged parrot?" He would continue to spin a yarn out of thin air.

The next day in school the Craddock children's history recital was colorful to say the least, much to the consternation of the teacher.

Recalling stories for use in sermons is not difficult. I thumb through my file of stories periodically just to refresh my memory of what is in the file. I make a point of not thumbing through the file when I am trying to come up with a story for a specific sermon. With general familiarity of the stories occasionally refreshed, I am able to meditate on the text and draw a suitable story like a magnet.

I know I am in trouble if I am in phase three, the creation phase, and I start looking through the story file. I will not say I never do it. I can say I rarely have good results when I look in the file for some story to fit the sermon. I find myself guilty of "shoehorning" into the sermon a story that does not fit. The text determines the message and the message determines the stories. When we give the story prime consideration, the process is reversed. We become guilty of letting the rhetorical device of story determine the message and the message distorting the text. I find it far better not to use a story than to force one to fit. To create one is better than going on an expedition through the story file.

Mainline church members today hunger and thirst for authentic religious experiences. That hunger may now be making moments of *kerygma* the base upon which to build revitalized congregations. The most frequent opportunity for most people to experience *kerygma* is in preaching. It is the golden thread in the fabric of church renewal. The visible, valuable and "vitalizing" power of preaching can model story weaving that gives substance to our congregation's teaching and learning, gives depth to our fellowship and restores energy and passion to our witness and service.

Chapter 7

Weaving Stories That Enliven Learning, Fellowship, and Witness and Service

Stories revitalize congregations.

God persistently reaches toward the church with the creative touch of new life in the stories of the church. Stories work by bringing alive individuals who bring the congregation to life. Stories work by helping congregations discover that they are woven into an ancient pattern of storytellers bringing alive the people of God with their yarns. The yarns are yet there to be told, to be listened to, to stir hope within us, to let us glimpse a God who would make our present life and witness an exciting episode in an ongoing story of new life.

An almost inexhaustible source of stories exists in the people of the congregation. Our task as church leaders is to help individual members and groups discover and share from the repertoire of their own stories. All that the church does is enlivened by the ongoing process of becoming familiar with the warp of the biblical story and weaving into that story the yarns from life near and far. Prayer, worship, and preaching are essential in establishing the importance of the biblical story, as well as practicing and modeling story weaving.

The vivid colors and patterns of story weaving move from the prayer closet and sanctuary to form vivid patterns in the actions of the church. Story weaving revitalizes all that the congregation does. In the classroom, story weaving enlivens learning. In the fellowship hall and in homes, story weaving bonds persons into deep, caring relationships. Beyond the church the power of story weaving is felt in the church's witness and service.

Most story weaving will go on informally. We who have leadership responsibilities can celebrate those times of revitalization that we do not even hear about. We can also enhance our congregation's vitality by structuring story weaving into the gathered life of the church. This chapter will offer specific suggestions for four areas of the congregation's life: learning, fellowship, and witness and service.

LEARNING

Staking a New Claim in Oklahoma

Granny Pritchard paid an uninvited visit to vacation church school every summer. The teachers were always disconcerted because they never knew the day or hour when Granny Pritchard would disrupt their lesson plan. It was often at a most inconvenient time such as when they finally had the children settled and the filmstrip projector working. The children would be absorbed in "Davey and Goliath" when a cane would tap on the door.

Every year Granny would go from door to door down the halls of the church with the children in her wake like the Pied Piper on parade. She would take them to the sanctuary and seat them around the chancel. There she would tell them of the day a line was drawn along the northern border of Oklahoma and the settlers lined up their wagons. Then someone shot off a gun that signaled the start of the mad scramble to stake out claims of Oklahoma land.

Granny went on to tell the story of the children's great grandparents driving a stake in each of the four corners on that very spot. They staked a claim for a church.

Christian education is the church passing on the tribal lore. It is drawing people into the clan so that they know its way of life and are proud to be part of the clan. Every year Granny passed along one of the important stories of tribal lore. She told of staking a claim for the church in Oklahoma. In telling the story she restaked a claim for the church in Oklahoma. She claimed for the church the lives of the children.

We are claimed by the power of stories. Educational settings are most suitable places for weaving our stories.

J. Cy Rowell, professor of religious education at Brite Divinity School, addresses the issue of the future of Sunday schools in mainline congregations.

At the children's level there will be classes, but the emphasis will be on hearing and experiencing the stories of the faithful community. This means Bible stories—not for the purpose of conversion or moralistic instruction, but for familiarizing children with the heritage of the Christian community. Highly decorated rooms, creative activities, lots of music and art, and moments of worship will be needed, all under the careful attention of warm and loving adults. The test of success will not be how many Bible verses the third grader can recite but whether she will say, "This is my church and I like to go to it."[23]

Education among children is, to use the metaphor of this book, putting into place the warp of Scripture and Tradition. Those stories of the warp can be used for a lifetime of weaving.

Adult classes are often attended more from need for intimate caring fellowship than from interest in being instructed. The class is a place where adults can know they are cared for by a religious community and a place where they discover a community with whom they share religious experiences. Sometimes learning may even occur. In the class, adults are continually reclaimed by the Christian clan.

Story weaving in most settings will be one method among many. Story weaving will take place along with lecture, discussion, panel, film viewing. Conceivably an adult class would do a story weaving exercise eight or ten times a year. I want to suggest one adult class that can continually use story weaving. I suggest a Bible study church school class based on the lectionary.

The lectionary class is a setting where persons come to "talk the text" that is the focal point of the church's life for the week. The text is used in prayer by the pastor (see Chapter 6) and others (see Chapter 4). It is at the center of the congregation's worship for the week (see Chapters 5 and 6). In class it becomes the warp of a small group's fellowship, religious experience, and learning.

The sessions follows an outline of three parts: 1. A fifteen-minute presentation of interpretive information, 2. Ten minutes for silent reflection and writing, 3. Twenty minutes for sharing stories. Times can be adjusted to fit the needs of the individual groups.

Let me offer a little more detailed help for the segments of the session. Early in the week before the session the preacher and the teacher of the class need to be in touch for the teacher to know the lection selected for the sermon for the coming Sunday. Even better is to get the information further in advance. The teacher then will do the research in the commentaries for the ten- to fifteen-minute presentation to the class.

I recommend the following outline for doing the research and presenting it to the class.

–the type of literature
–first readers and their concerns and issues being addressed by the text
–message of the writer to those concerns and issues
–meaning of key words
–map study of places mentioned, identity of characters
–comparison of translations

While preparing, the teacher may also use the text as a way to be aware of members of the class and to pray for them. The text becomes a prayer resource as well as an item of fascination for research. Peter Ainslee, early twentieth-century ecumenist, observed, ". . . the Sunday-school teacher who has prayed well has studied well, for while a prepared lesson is essential, a prepared heart is even more essential."[24]

The session can begin with greetings, news of the class, and a chance for people to visit. Next the lection is read aloud with each one following in his or her own Bible. The leader then presents the facts behind the text as outlined above. Some clarifying questions and discussion may follow. The second part of the session is for guided, quiet reflection on the text. This story weaving begins in the silence. Before the quiet time you, the leader, may offer suggestions. "In the quiet, think of what we have read and talked about. Think of the text as the word of God seeking us. What experiences do you remember or know about from others that are brought to mind by the text? When you come to a specific memory, take your mind off of 'scanner' and let yourself relive that memory. Bring back specific people, places, times, events. You may want to jot down a note or two about the story you remember, or you may want to paraphrase the text as you perceive it to be a word of God written for you. You may wish to write a prayer of concern or thanksgiving about the people and the incident you remember. We will be taking ten minutes of quiet to weave one of your stories into one of God's stories."

At the conclusion of the quiet time, invite people to share by listening and talking within groups of four. Always the rule applies of no pressure to talk. People are to share only what they wish to share.

The session can close with general conversation and prayer. It is also a good idea to work ahead and let class members know the text for the next session.

We learn in three ways: cognition, experience, and reflection. In cognition we receive information and it becomes a road map for understanding and comprehending. The mini-lecture on the text adds to the learner's store of information. Experience involves body, mind, and emotion. In the experience of hearing the stories of others, we involve our feelings for the person who shares as well as the story that is shared. We feel what the story-teller feels: angry or helpless, or hopeful or forgiven. We often feel united or bonded with that person as a story awakens another of our own stories and the two weave together. In reflection we take time to ponder cognitive information and experience, and we identify learnings and values to instruct and guide the way we live. In the quiet of the session suggested above, we reflect, we appropriate learnings and values as we weave our stories into the biblical story. In the venture of story weaving, learning becomes wholistic and the church's education becomes vital.

Some preachers raise questions about the lectionary-based church school class. "How can my sermon be interesting if the class has already been through the material of the text?" The answer may surprise us. The sermon is more interesting, not less, because the listener has already studied the text. The Bible is the whole congregation's Bible. The preacher is not the dispenser of the Word, but the focal point of the people of God engaged in breaking open the Word. The worshipers who have participated in the lectionary class receive the sermon as active participants in preaching. They are already interested. Interest doesn't have to be won. They are already active in engaging the text to let it interweave in a transforming way with their own lives.

An experiment I conducted confirms that preaching is enhanced when a class studies the lectionary text. The sermon printed in Appendix B was preached in three settings. The experiment had a congregation of both ordained and non-ordained persons use Luke 24:35-48 as a prayer resource in silence and

109

solitude. Then they met for an hour in classes to go through the text as outlined in the model session above. The classes then assembled for worship in which I preached on the same text. The congregation's emotional and mental involvement in the moment of preaching was powerfully evident in tears, laughter, discussion after the service. I used as control groups two congregations who had not engaged the text prior to worship. The only change in the sermon was a reduction and simplification of the material about Luke the writer in the introduction. One congregation was almost 100 percent clergy. The other congregation was a typical Sunday morning gathering. In both the control groups, the sermon was received with appreciation. However, these congregations' participation was much less active and intense than that of the group in the experiment. Preachers, your best congregations on Sunday mornings are the ones who nod in recognition and familiarity to your sermon. They participate in the story weaving of preaching in a vital and "vitalizing" way because engaging the biblical story is for them and you a shared enterprise.

FELLOWSHIP

Arlone shares a story.

 ### No One Came, Until . . .

"I lost my best friend and no one came; it didn't seem to matter to anyone. When I lost my Dad, I was devastated but no one came. Then my neighbor lost her Mother, and even though she, too, belonged to our church, no one came for her either. The pastor came, but we really felt the need for other people to share with us at this time. I began to wonder if there were a lot of people like me. I felt the world was crying and no one was listening.

"I became very angry at my church and called on Pastor Rick. He told me he had just the program for me, Caring Ministry. I had no idea what it was when my neighbor and I went with him. I learned it is more important to minister to the soul than to fill the pew. We learned that every one of us has a story and each story is different. We need to listen to each other's story and

110

convey genuine caring. Sometimes we hear very happy stories . . .
(also) there are many sad stories that need to be listened to.

"I have really enjoyed it. We have held new babies, drunk a
lot of coffee, shared some of the very best cookies made, we have
visited children, teenagers, young families, and "not so young"
families. We have visited shut-ins and people in the hospital and
nursing homes. It has been really something. My teammate and I
try to make one call per week. We have learned a lot about
ourselves. We are not the only people who need to hear caring
from the church."[25]

With a little sensitivity and effort, congregations can be places
of love and caring. We live in a time almost desperate for love and
caring as reflected in the first part of Arlone's story. "No one
came." "It didn't seem to matter." "I felt like the world was crying
and no one was listening." Groups such as Caring Ministry help
train and support members of the church in structured programs
of caring.*

Uprootedness, disconnectedness, and social fragmentation
are signs that basic human social needs are often no longer met
by society in North America. Lifelong residency in one neighborhood in which people visited over the back fence and watched
from front porch swings as neighbors strolled by on leisurely
evening walks is as obsolete in most places as talking to "central"
to make a telephone call. The need to be known by name and
valued as an individual remains.

What an opportunity congregations have to be cells or groups
of cells where people are individually known and loved as they
share life stories. In congregations the human community is
scaled down to individual dimensions. The church is a natural
place for people who need people to come together. Congregations are settings where individuals achieve personal recognition,
share experiences, find assurance of emotional and other support
and develop enduring friendships. The church is a place that
benefits the community and individuals by offering the contradictory values of stability and diversity. "Society changes, the com-

---

*Recommended resource: For more information on Caring Ministry contact
Kenneth Mitchell, Suite 2A, 2180 Garnet Avenue, San Diego, CA 92109.

munity changes, people change, I change, yet the church endures and I am part of it," spoke one forty-year member. In the fullest sense, church is home, the place of the extended family offering intimate care to its own.

Three points of integration are needed for most persons to maintain an enduring, valued relationship with a congregation. 1. The congregation must be a place of personal friendships. 2. It is to be a place where members are aware of having religious experiences, encounters with God. 3. Members need also to be part of a shared enterprise of value, that is, they are to be a part of a mission that, they sense, is greater than they are.

The church at its best responds to those social and religious needs of individuals by bringing them together to know Christ's love for them in the love they give and receive from each other. That fellowship, *koinonia*, is so powerful that it is "membered," put together, bonded by Christ's love into the body of Christ. That love is directed inward in the sense that individuals thrive on knowing they are loved. That love is intimate in that it is given and received personally from other members. That love is also outreaching. Christ's love cannot be confined to an "in" group, but lavishly breaks loose to suffer the world's pain with the world, and is to be spent in ministering to the world God created and loves through the church.

The Christian community is our meeting place. It is our place of receiving love that brings wholeness. It is our place of giving love that brings wholeness to others. It is our place from which we are sent in order to risk offering hope and wholeness to those beyond the fellowship.

The front door to Christian community is simple hospitality. The words, "Good morning, Susan," when she walks into the church are an ordinary courtesy, but they are more. Those words are the beginning of a series of words and gestures that create Christian community. The coffee hour is not just the coffee hour. It is the first place of contact. Later, stories can be shared and lives will be woven together.

Fellowship in the congregation is the weaving together of individual lives with the gospel into a fabric of Christian community. Again, the gospel is the warp. Persons with their stories are the woof. When the fabric is well woven, it is beautiful to look at and touch with its great variety of color and the uniqueness of personalities and personal histories. It is also strong. People hear each other's pain. People come into intense conflict. Yet, the pain and the conflict do not rip apart the fabric. Lives are held together by the gospel.

The Vote

The powerful people of the congregation met to discuss what they were going to do about the pastor. She seemed a misfit. They complained that all they heard were sermons on social action. She was too liberal for them. It was time to do something. They had been patient for five years. They agreed that their decision must be unanimous. They would stand together in working with the pastor or in asking her to resign.

An evening of anguished discussion followed. Finally, exhausted, they reached a consensus. They would ask the pastor to resign.

One of the group reminded them that they had to have Frank's consent. The vote had to be unanimous. Frank's wife had just died so he was not at the meeting. The group appointed three people to report to Frank and to win his consent. No trouble was expected. Frank was the pastor's most outspoken critic.

Two weeks later the three sat in Frank's living room and gave a detailed report on their meeting. They asked Frank to make the vote unanimous. He thought for a moment, then spoke quietly. "I have been the pastor's strongest opponent. There is no one in the church who disagrees with her more than I do. But you need to know that I also love our pastor and I won't vote against her.

"You see, twelve hours before my wife died the pastor was holding her hand. Twelve hours after my wife died she was holding my hand. I cannot be against anyone who would love a critic that much."

How do those of us who are trusted to lead the congregation help it realize its full value and power? How is the simple method of story weaving helpful in letting the congregation live up to its calling as a community where Christ is known and shared?

Most of the story weaving will happen spontaneously. People will share out of their need to be known and loved, and out of their desire to return love to those who hear their stories with care. We who lead have three responsibilities: 1. To oversee programs that let people share naturally, 2. To provide settings in which sharing is intentionally based in the gospel and 3. To see that all the people of the congregation have a shepherd with whom they may share.

We oversee programs where people share naturally. Choirs, women's groups, men's groups, youth groups, study groups, action groups, recreational groups are all settings where people come together with the opportunity to have their lives woven into community. As leaders, we look over the entire range of such groups to make sure that enough of them are provided and that every one in the congregation knows about them. I recommend having one group for every sixteen participating members.

Fellowship is not just the social life of the congregation. We who lead are to offer planned times when people's stories are woven together based on the gospel. People of the church need and expect experiences that are explicitly religious. Settings for this are the lectionary church school class and the lectors' groups already described. Occasional times of story weaving can occur in committees, fellowship, and other groups with regular meetings.

An annual prayer retreat is an excellent time to do story weaving. The material in Chapter 4 is designed for times of solitude in the retreat. Small-group story weaving described in Chapter 3 is an excellent way to bond lives together based on the gospel. The use of intercessory prayer for members of the congregation further extends the weaving. One way to do this uses memory and imagination. You as leader have the retreatants relax. You tell them that they will be praying using the backs of their eyelids as screens on which they will see persons you will suggest. You then offer a description and encourage the people at prayer to picture a person who fits that description. Give enough time to let the people sense the presence of those for whom they pray in silence. You lead the group in a unison prayer aloud, "I surround you with the love of God that is in Christ Jesus." You then move on through a list of descriptions for persons to use in picturing people. Each time they offer silent intercession, then pray together, "I surround you with the love of God that is in Christ Jesus." You conclude the prayer time by speaking for the group a prayer of thanksgiving for all of the different kinds of people in your congregation. You offer descriptions, not names. A list of descriptions can include the person most appreciative of the church, a person in great personal pain, the hardest worker in the church, someone who has dropped out of the church, a favorite child (tell the people it is all right to picture their own children and grandchildren), the church comedian, the newest member of the church. You can create your own list of descriptions for guiding intercessions at prayer retreats.

Our responsibilities as leaders include providing shepherds for all members of the church. Some members are gifted in social relationships. Others soon fade into the wallpaper if some help is not given. Often the ones who most need and want to be known and loved are the same ones who have the most difficulty in reaching out on their own to cultivate relationships. The goal of the fellowship of the church is to see that all the members are known and called by name, recognized when they are present, and told they are missed when they are absent. Shepherds help all people, especially the overlooked, be a part of a community firmly woven together in the gospel.*

When we think through fellowship, *koinonia*, we use some high-flown words: bonded together in Christ, a community of caring and sharing, participation or "membered" into the body of Christ. Those words only point to a reality that we know fully in the touch of grace by a friend in Christ. We know and extend the reality of *koinonia* in the stories we remember and tell, stories of caring in the congregation that are woven into the biblical story.

Lyle heard the story of "Paul's Farewell." That story from the Bible then brought to mind one of his memorable moments as a shepherd of the congregation.

The Elders at Paul's Farewell

The apostle Paul was driven by visions of extending the church. On to Rome! On to Spain! His detractors interfered with building his vision. How can building stones be laid when only one hand can be used for the work and the other must be used to fend off the attackers?

Paul decided to stop the process. He would go to Palestine and settle the dispute through litigation. He set sail.

His ship came to a rest stop on the island of Miletus in the Aegean Sea not far from the large cosmopolitan city of Ephesus.

---

*Recommended resource: "Disciples Eldership" by Peter M. Morgan, available from Christian Board of Publication, P.O. Box 179, St. Louis, MO 63166.

Paul thought of all the small churches of Ephesus that he had helped found and had supported. He called for their elders to visit him on Miletus.

We can imagine he greeted the elders with great affection. He then spoke to them in serious tones. "I know that all you among whom I have gone preaching the kingdom will see my face no more. . . . I did not shrink from declaring to you the whole counsel of God. Take heed to yourselves and to all the flock, in which the Holy Spirit has made you overseers, to care for the church of God which he obtained with the blood of his own Son" (Acts 20:25, 27-28).

After Paul spoke he and the elders wept and prayed together. The elders would never again see Paul. They would remember his charge to them as shepherds to care for the church of God.

Lyle remembered his ministry as one charged to be a shepherd.

An Elder at Tommy's Farewell

"Tommy knew the lonely isolation that comes with blindness and with the death of friends as the years advanced him to old age. Tommy and I had been friends most of my life and I tried to keep in touch.

"One Sunday another elder and I had Tommy on our list of shut-ins that we were to visit with the Lord's Supper. We knocked on the door and heard Tommy's, 'Come in.' When we got inside, Tommy, with hand extended, asked who we were. Without a word I took his hand. He said, 'It's Lyle.' He told my friend later that he always recognized my touch because, 'Something always passes between us when we touch.'

"The Lord's Supper had special meaning that day and also a few days later. I heard then that Tommy had died. Tommy's hand had gone from my hand to God's hand. I knew something special had passed between them when they touched."

WITNESS AND SERVICE

Stories told inside the church have impact even on the world outside the church. The vitality of the congregation's witness and service to the world is enhanced when those who are sent from the church have been together sharing stories.

Christ reaches to the world through two hands of the church. One hand is the church's witness: evangelism. The other hand is the church's service: prophetic works and deeds of compassion.

Hair Rollers and Contagious Faith

As a young pastor, I once became frustrated because the congregation was having a difficult time filling its slate of deacons for an upcoming election. I took my worries to the elders. "Who is going to do all that work for the church?"

The elders took their young minister to school that night. They instructed me that if a deacon is truly a servant, the world needs that service as much or more than the church. "Are you suggesting that Bill give up his position on the Boy Scout Council, that Hank give up his Christian presence on the police auxiliary, that Floyd resign the county board of supervisors, and that Lu give up her one day a week of volunteering to go to the nursing homes to set hair so that we can have a full slate of deacons?"

I'll remember that lesson for the rest of my life. Whenever I think of deacons, I think of Lu Schlotterback taking a strong and contagious faith along with the hair rollers and lotions. She helped those who needed courage and hope to have a faith.

The witnesses and the servants are courageous people who constantly spend themselves in tiring, discouraging, sometimes dangerous work. Making evangelistic calls in the community or sensitizing the community to the issue of nuclear disarmament, or tutoring kids from poor neighborhoods is demanding, often draining away resolve. The church is called to be the place of replenishment. Story weaving enlivens the witness and service of the church.

The witnesses and servants must be determined to reach beyond the church with the gospel. That necessary determination has a risk. The passion to serve can be so consuming that we who witness and serve in the world only pay attention to the demands of our serving. We neglect caring for ourselves, replenishing our strength. When we serve only out of the goodness of our hearts, we become burnt out. Eventually we and the cause we serve suffer when we do not look to maintaining our vitality. We become unraveled from the warp of the gospel, unwoven from the life-giving stories of others who share our mission. The church is the place of celebrating with the stories of victory and being healed as we share stories of pain. We are made strong again by reweaving the torn threads of our venture into the strong fabric of the church's larger story.

A risk awaits us in returning to the church. Outside the fellowship is the risk of hardship. Inside is the risk of ease. The fellowship of persons who share our concerns for the world often is so refreshing that we have difficulty breaking loose to return again to our witness and service in the world. When we see that we have replaced our witnessing with talk and stories about witnessing, then it is time to laugh at ourselves and move out again. We can laugh, "It looks as if I have fallen into the huddle heresy again." We can go out again even though we may be afraid. We know that people in the church will be there later to hear our stories, share theirs, and reconnect us with the life-restoring story of the gospel.

The gospel story itself teaches us as witnesses and servants to practice the rhythm of spending ourselves in ministry in the world and then retreating to share the stories that replenish.

Jesus must have been apprehensive as he sent his "trainees" into the world. He teamed the disciples into pairs and addressed the mixed anxiety and eagerness that they and he must have felt. "The harvest is plentiful." "I send you out as lambs in the midst of wolves" (Luke 10:2-3).

Later when they returned, both trainer and trainees were pleased. What stories they must have told! "Lord, even the demons are subject to us in your name" (v. 17). They celebrated their victories together.

Jesus then continued to prepare his disciples. He used a story. He taught them about being a neighbor when they were on the road, away from the safety of friends. "A man was going down from Jerusalem to Jericho, and he fell among robbers . . . a Samaritan . . . came to where he was; and when he saw him, he had compassion . . ." Who was the neighbor? "Go and do likewise" (Luke 10:25-37).

Not all the disciples' attempts at mission brought celebration. The pain of failure also drew them together, drew them toward Jesus. Jesus had been away at prayer. As he returned, a man knelt before him saying that the disciples had been unable to help his epileptic son. Jesus healed the boy. The disciples privately came to Jesus to learn from their failure. "Why could we not cast it out?" (Matthew 17:19). Jesus spoke to them of faith.

Witness and service can be tiring, lonely work. Most of us need people with whom we celebrate victories and learn from defeats. Story weaving helps keep our witness and service vital. Let me offer two examples.

The apostle Andrew is the evangelist of the Twelve. His story becomes warp into which we who are witnesses today weave our stories. In a time of training or renewal, divide the evangelism callers into three groups. Assign each group a passage on Andrew: John 1:35-42; John 6:1-12; or John 12:20-22. One person in each group reads the assignment aloud while others listen for answers to three questions you have listed. "What is the action? What is the high moment in the passage? What do you guess are the feelings of the people involved?" The small groups discuss the questions. As a total group, they share a summary of the three texts, then continue the discussion. "What is happening to Andrew as a person in this experience? What guidelines enabled Andrew to do what he did? What do we guess motivated his actions?" Evangelists can practice their listening and sharing skills by forming into pairs. One person portrays Andrew and is interviewed by the other. The whole group can then discuss learnings from being Andrew and interviewing Andrew. Next give them time for quiet reflection. List questions that people may use in their reflections. "Where are my experiences similar to Andrew's and different from Andrew's? What does Andrew's story say to me about my work as an evangelist? In what ways can I be like Andrew? What qualities did he have that are like some of mine? What did he do that I can do?" Invite people to share with a partner what they would enjoy having the other person know.*

Evangelism is weaving others' stories into the gospel story in such a way that their lives are transformed. Those lives are woven into God's story as it was given in the gospels and as it continuing in the church. Many skills are involved including story listening and sharing of faith stories. Our effectiveness depends upon a contagious faith kept vital through our continuing to discover through story weaving how our stories are part of God's story.

Servant ministry takes many forms. We serve as individuals and in groups. We set hair in the nursing home. We serve on the city council. We are volunteers in Scouts. We give time to our church's "Helping Hand Store." We advocate issues of peace and justice. As we spend ourselves in ministries, we need to maintain vitality in service by being with others to connect to their stories and to renew the vision. Transforming energy comes from being explicitly and intentionally Christian as together we weave our story into the biblical story and as we pray together.

The following example of story weaving for servants comes from a group seeking to be connected with Christians from the global church who suffer for their faith. We open the Bible to our story as written in 1 Peter and set the loom with the yarn of the warp.

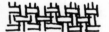 ## A Letter to the Gentiles

The apostle Peter, leader of the Jewish Christians, dictates a letter to Silvanus. (Peter's limited knowledge of Greek made Silvanus a near necessity.) The letter is to be read by small groups of Gentile converts to Christianity in a remote part of the world in today's Turkey. Turning to Christianity has resulted in these Gentiles becoming newly made aliens living in their own land. They have aroused the suspicion and slander of their own people. Also we know the threat to them is becoming more intense. Soon after that time the Roman government began persecuting Christians.

Peter writes to them. He uses terms such as "fiery ordeal" (1 Peter 4:12), "suffer various trials" (1:6), "when you are abused" (3:16). He writes to them of their suffering, their adversity.

*Recommended resources: "Order of Andrew" Leaders' Cassette Album, "My Journal" and *Gracious Contagion*, available from Christian Board of Publication, P.O. Box 179, St. Louis, MO 63166.

Peter is not a detached supporter, cheering encouragement from offstage. Peter too is a fellow-sufferer who soon will hang dead from a cross. But, his letter points them not to the shadow of his own cross, but to a cross of a suffering Savior in whom to find courage and glory.

The weaving begins. After telling the story of 1 Peter using the above story or another version created from your own research, help people discover the letter first as written to them and then as a letter to pass along to others. Here is one way of proceeding.

God seeks us through the biblical story. Have people prayerfully enter a time of silence with their Bibles and writing material. In the silence they are to remember times in their own lives of deep distress or suffering. They may want to specifically recall a time in ministry when they were hurt. Many of them have lived past those moments without ever having them healed. As they become aware of their own stories of pain, have them turn to four lessons from 1 Peter and silently read them as if they were written personally to them: 2:19-25; 4:12-14, 19; 2:9-10; 5:1-5. After some time of reflection have them imagine that the apostle Peter had heard about them and was writing a letter to them. Have them write that letter from Peter to them. After the silence you may wish to have free time in which people may or may not choose to share their letter with another.

The weaving goes on. The followers of Jesus Christ are woven into each others' lives across national, cultural, and denominational borders. Peter, head of the "Jewish denomination," wrote to the Gentile converts. People today also suffer for their faith. From your reading or from correspondence with your denominational offices, put together the stories of one or two Christians from the global church who have recently suffered for their faith. Often those stories will be of torture and imprisonment by governments because church leaders have sought to protect the human rights of their people. The stories are not pleasant, but you must be specific. This is not to be about people in general who suffer. Indicate that their stories are to be woven into our story. The church of Jesus Christ is to be a whole fabric. Again have people enter the silence with their Bibles and writing material. They are to keep prayerfully before them the people you have spoken of as they read 1 Peter 1:6-7; 1:22-25; 5:1-4; 5:6-11.

They are to pray for the persons in the stories you have told. Then they are to write a letter of solidarity and support and mutual faith to one of the persons in their prayer just as Peter wrote to the Gentiles long ago.

The letters can be sent to the source where you learned the story. Suggest that the helpful letters be selected to send on to the person prayed for by your group. Some letters may not communicate support and may need to be omitted.

Here are two letters woven from personal stories interacting with 1 Peter, then sent on to be woven into the lives of a pastor in South Africa who suffered.

Pastor _____

I am sitting in a comfortable chair, in an air-conditioned building on a Saturday afternoon. Peter Morgan has just shared with us some of the suffering you've endured. I am no longer comfortable here.

My thoughts the last few months have been centered on my difficulty with an alcoholic husband, and a handicapped child. Poor me. Poor me, indeed! My suffering and that of my family is so inconsequential after knowing what you've been through.

The Scriptures have taught me that our God does not want us to suffer. Satan, however, has other ideas. I cannot know how you've found strength to keep your eyes on the Lord and not succumb to anger and rebellion.

It is not in my power to take away your suffering nor can you take away mine. Since knowing about you, I can now face my trials with a new freshness and much less anger. I know God is with me in my everyday problems. I pray that you feel his presence in your sometimes overwhelming sufferings.
A Friend in Christ.

Dear Pastor _____

Greetings in the name of our Savior, Jesus Christ.

How great is your faith and how sure you can be of our love and prayers for the "living faith" you have shown in the ordeal you underwent.

It is difficult I'm sure for you to believe that we care and for us all to keep our faith strong in days of such persecution to those working for liberation of God's people.

We send to you through our constant and fervent prayers strength and hope to see you through these times.

May God grant you peace and give you our love through prayer. May his love surround you and protect you as you continue on your journey of ministry.

Agape.

The church comes to life when the base of its experience is the *kerygma*, shared good news. That base is discovered in stories of Scripture and Tradition heard and seen in prayer, worship, and preaching. Those stories can weave into our own experiences. In the weaving, our congregation's teaching and learning, fellowship, and witness and service will be transformed.

The *kerygma* is synonymous with Peter's sermon at Pentecost, the day the church was created. Peter pointed to the hope of people in the past as he quoted Joel. ". . . God declares, that I will pour out my Spirit upon all flesh, and your sons and daughters shall prophesy, and your young men shall see visions, and your old men shall dream dreams . . ." (Acts 2:17).

In that powerful moment of creation the past was woven into the future. Old prophecy awakened new prophecy. The old dreams awakened the new dreams. The old visions awakened the new visions. God's life-giving Spirit created the church. Now is also a powerful moment of creation when the past can be woven into the future. The old prophecy can awaken new prophecy. The old dreams can awaken the new dreams. The old visions can awaken the new visions, and God's life-giving Spirit can *re*create the church.

Conclusion

Church historian Martin E. Marty speaks of revitalization in mainline churches. "You're dead if you don't aspire to offering a nurturing experience. There is no such thing as religious revitalization among people who don't experience. You can live off experience through interpretation and action, but that's a one-generation phenomenon, and you have to keep replenishing it. So, while you can't just say, let's have a burning bush and have it burn, or let's have a still, small voice, and have a still, small voice; you can at least say, 'if the bush is burning we're going to notice it and if the voice is speaking, we're going to hear it.' There are things that can be done."[26]

"There are things that can be done." This book is my contribution to the things that can be done. God's life-giving Spirit persistently reaches for the church to offer new life. We look to Scripture and Tradition not to romanticize some golden age of the past, but to stand speechless and awe-filled before the miracle of God creating and re-creating community. Our speechless awe is gently nudged to attentive listening then exuberant laughter as we hear the stories of God's people and recognize them as our stories. We are a story-formed community. The stories, the listening, the laughing, the retelling help us celebrate the golden age of our own today and tomorrow.

Appendix A: Stories

Appendix B: A Sermon

The development of this sermon is described in Chapter 6. It was preached before a congregation of ordained and non-ordained church leaders attending a seminar on worship, prayer, and preaching. Members of the congregation had used the text for prayer in solitude and had engaged in dialogue on the text in a church school class prior to coming to worship.

"Fish Bones on the Rim of the Plate"
Luke 24:35-48

I take us to the writing desk of Luke this morning. On the writing stand before us we find an almost finished parchment of the life of Jesus. A stack of papyrus notes on the life of the apostles awaits Luke's attention. There is also an inkstand and pens and a parchment of the Gospel of Mark rolled open to the ending lines.

The enterprise of writing is more than equipment. It is the soul of the writer. What of the writer Luke? He is a biographer and theologian for whom knowledge is all important. Ignorance is sin. Remember in Luke's writing Jesus asks for forgiveness for those who crucified him. "Father, forgive them, they *KNOW* not what they do." *Knowledge* of the truth is the discovery of salvation. So Luke tells us at the beginning of the Gospel that "it seems good to write an orderly account . . . that you may *KNOW* the truth concerning these things." The whole enterprise is "to know"; knowledge is for salvation.

Luke's first challenge is as a biographer. Through story and a few clips of dialogue he wants us to *KNOW* the personality and character of Jesus.

Imagine the deliberations of Luke as he comes to this midpoint in his writing. The task of the moment is to put in writing the resurrection appearance of Jesus to the disciples. He has written of the women finding the empty tomb. The open parchment awaits his words. In the creative struggle Luke is searching for words to tell of disciples who were soul-dead and who at the touch of a risen Christ, who they thought was dead, come alive themselves. This seems a decisive midpoint in the story. It's the moment when the disciples come alive to begin their mighty acts through which God's Spirit births and builds the church. Luke is a biographer.

Second, Luke is a theologian. Luke is troubled by a complex theological issue that is seething in the church. How could God be in Jesus when Jesus died? Is God known in Jesus real?

It is hard to fathom God as an infant nursing at Mary's breast. Hard to fathom God as a helpless infant being diapered. But it is scandalously unthinkable for God to act helpless before sadistic soldiers with hammer and nails intended for human flesh—God's hands! Scandalously unthinkable for God to act helpless before cynical politicians. God's dying is unthinkable.

Luke has Mark's Gospel open before him. These last lines of Mark tell virtually nothing of Jesus' resurrection appearances, just as the first lines told nothing of Jesus' conception and birth.

Luke is aware that Mark's silence contributes to the controversy in the church over how could God really be in Jesus. Jesus died on the cross. It's not possible for God to die. God would not be God if God died!

Speculation runs through the church. Some are saying that Jesus had no body. He was a hallucination to help us think of God. Others speculate that God avoided the problem of dying when Jesus died. By excellent timing he came into the body of Jesus after the messiness of birth. He left the body of Jesus before it expired. (Our forebears of the first century weren't as "simple" as we sometimes assume. I find this a complex theological issue.) Luke the biographer/theologian—for whom ignorance was sin—writes "that you may know the truth concerning . . . [these] things" (1:3-4).

Luke ponders—"How to say it? I have to tell of Jesus' appearance to the disciples. Mark is not much help. How am I going to say it?"

He rolls open the scroll and reads yesterday's last written words describing the Emmaus road. "Then they told what had happened on the road (to Emmaus), and how he was known to them in the breaking of bread" (24:35).

Luke picks up the pen and begins to write of God in human flesh in Jesus Christ who had suffered and died and now who came to touch the disciples and to send them into life fully alive, a mission fully alive.

AN AMBER ROOM

"The eleven gathered together and those who were with them" (v. 33). In ten scant words Luke sketches the background. We fill in the details, paint in the colors. Ten scant words: "The eleven gathered together and those who were with them."

The scene is familiar to all of us, especially pastors who have been in dozens of living rooms with families after a funeral. Here is a drawing together, a huddling in common hurt. Yet each one is strangely alone with his or her own regrets, doubts, guilt, aching loss.

Luke invites us into a very deep, private moment in the life of the disciples. Amber walls have been sooted by oil lamps. The varying tones of the amber walls are dimly lit now by those lamps. The light also illumines the amber skin of sad Palestinian faces.

Here in a corner a small group talks quietly of sunny days in Galilee and Jesus' words, "Follow me" (5:27). Unsaid is the thought, "Would I have followed if I had known it would hurt so much now?"

There one of them sits alone and remembers the beautiful experience on the mountain of transfiguration. It was about then that everything started to change. Jesus started talking of being delivered into the hands of men. They began making their way to Jerusalem. Maybe that was the point when they went wrong (9:28-29, 44, 51).

Into the silence of the amber room another follower ventures the words "and they crucified him." The unspoken reply in all their hearts was, "Could I have prevented it . . . what did I do wrong?"

The group is leaderless, lifeless, lost.

You've been with friends in that amber room. George had not driven by the cemetery near his home for two years without shedding a tear, sighing, or experiencing an unexpressed inner ache. George's Sara died two years ago. Two years, and George still wasn't back to living. He tried playing golf again, but to please the friends who worried about him, not for the enjoyment. He went to work. But work was putting in time. No exhilaration came from the challenges, no satisfactions from the accomplishments.

George's route to work, to church, to the shops went right by the cemetery where Sara was buried. For two years George drove by that cemetery every day and he had yet to drive by without a tear, a sigh or an unexpressed inner ache. You have been with friends in the amber light of loss.

You've sat in that amber room yourself, have you not? Was it the time you were moving to a new position and as the moving van pulled out you remembered a younger, fresher, more energetic you? The moving vans were coming in that day instead of leaving. Now you think of more recent painful days. As you pack the boxes and clean out your desk, the old dreams are only mocking phantoms in an amber room.

You've sat in that amber room. Was it a divorce? . . . sickness? . . . death of a parent or child or mate? . . . vocational burnout?

We've sat with the disciples in that amber room and the music in our souls was not "Lead On, O King Eternal," it was "Nobody Knows the Trouble I've Seen."

A TOUCHABLE JESUS

How can God wipe the tears from our eyes if we've never wept? Especially in our times of tears we go back to being child-like in our need for tangible signs of security. We need a touchable Jesus. We know that truth as we remember the feel of our mother's hand on our fevered foreheads when we were ten years old and her words, "Would a little ice cream help?" We know that truth from the trembling touch of hands with our beloved on our wedding day. We know it from the assuring touch of a friend who buys us a cup of coffee and speaks the right word when we are uncertain.

Something extraordinary happened to George. George got acquainted with Roberta. He awakened to her wit and her touch. But Roberta, surprisingly, compounded the problem.

There were still the drives by the cemetery. Now George was deeply troubled by feeling guilty that he may replace Sara with someone else. He felt disloyal to forty years of marriage and to Sara's memory. He felt he was unfaithful to the grief that had become deeply bonded to him in two years. George began to spend agonizing hours by Sara's grave. George would weep with joy when with Roberta, then would weep with guilt by Sara's grave.

One day a wise friend dropped by who had been through a similar experience. George was a little flustered. Sara was the one who knew what to do when company dropped in. But George managed to put on a pot of coffee and got a couple of Hostess cupcakes out of the freezer. Over the coffee cups and cupcake wrappers the friend reached out and took George's hand and said, "You know, George, it is because of Sara's love of forty years that you need and can fully give love to Roberta. It's OK to love and be loved." The friend for a moment became a touchable Jesus. "He was known in the breaking of bread" (24:35). George accepted the words but did not think about them until the next day. The words and his friend's touch came back as he drove past the cemetery and caught himself whistling. No tear, no sigh, no unexpressed inner ache. Life had begun again!

The Eleven had heard the women's report of the empty tomb. Luke tells us, "These words seemed to them an idle tale, and they did not believe them" (v. 11). Words were not enough.

Into the amber room a couple had come to say they had walked the Emmaus road with a risen Christ whom they recognized as he opened the Word to them and shared bread and wine. The couple's story had no effect (vs. 13-35). Words are not enough. Even eyewitness accounts aren't enough. When we hurt, we need a touchable Jesus.

The evangelist Luke now presents a risen Christ. He presents him into the amber room of the Eleven. He presents him to a church feuding over resurrection. He presents him to us. He presents him to the world that all may believe.

"See my hands, my feet . . . handle me." "A spirit has not flesh and bones as you see that I have" (v. 39). The disciples could not believe for joy. It was too good to be true. The animated Jesus asked for food. They brought him broiled fish. They could see the morsels of fish going into Jesus' mouth; they could see Jesus take the fish bones out of his mouth and place them on the side of the plate. He was not a phantom.

He was a touchable Jesus. "He was known to them in the breaking of bread."

Jesus then spoke to them of Scripture. "I am the same one who spoke to you before the cross. I am the same one spoken of in the law and the prophets and psalms. What is too good to be true, is true!" He was no God with a disappearing act. Jesus is the anointed of God, fully suffering in death, fully triumphant in Resurrection, and fully present now—a touchable Jesus.

Later the Eleven and we who gather with them could count the fish bones on the rim of his plate and see a little leftover wine in his chalice.

A young pastor came to that moment of his first conflict with his first congregation. The subject of the conflict was so small that it has now faded past the point of recall. But when he was twenty-seven years old the subject must not have seemed small for he still can remember the feelings of being afraid and lost. He called his regional minister and talked by phone. A couple of days later the phone rang and it was the regional minister. He said, "I'm in town to take you to lunch." The young minister never knew if he drove over just for him or if he was passing through. He doesn't remember what was said at lunch, but does remember the feelings. He was in the presence of a strong, good man of faith. He absorbed perspective on the problem, strength and faith. He needed a touchable Jesus—and at that moment his pastor became his touchable Jesus. That regional minister was Loren Lair of Iowa. I was the young minister. In my memory now is a picture: a table with the plates of a finished lunch—cups with the last drops of coffee in the bottom—plates with olive pits on the side. I remember another deeper picture of a table and plates with fish bones on the side—and a chalice with a little leftover wine. "He was known to them in the breaking of bread" (v. 35).

Oh, how we can thank God for those people in our lives who become so close that from time to time when we need them they become our touchable Jesus!

A TOUCH OF GRACE

After a pensive stroll around his desk Luke writes, "Repentance and forgiveness of sins should be preached in his name to all nations, beginning from Jerusalem" (v. 47). As we go to neighbors and nations alike, occasionally, wonder of wonders, we are surprised to discover we, too, become a touchable Jesus to someone. That is not an honor to be seized. We remember Paul's words: "Have this mind among yourselves, which is yours in Christ Jesus, who, though he was in the form of God, did not count equality with God a thing to be grasped, but emptied himself, taking the form of a servant, being born in the likeness of men" (Philippians 2:5-7).

It was an experience veiled in mystery. De Vee was a friend in Iowa who had moved to Cleveland. I had a stopover in the Cleveland airport one day and decided to call my old friend. No answer. The public address speaker announced that the flight to Chicago and Cedar Rapids was delayed. I walked over to Gate Twelve on the remote chance I would know someone going to Cedar Rapids. There sat De Vee bathed in amber light, quietly weeping. I went to her. We touched and talked. Later in the lunchroom I heard the reason for the tears. A daughter-in-law had forbidden contact between this mother and her son and grandchildren. As she finished her story, she reached over and touched my hand and said, "God sent you to me today." She needed a touchable Jesus that moment and I—filled with wonder—had been sent. I looked at the table in the airport restaurant and saw a bit of broken bread and I remembered another deeper picture of a table and plates and fish bones on the side and a chalice with a little leftover wine. "He was known to them in the breaking of bread" (Luke 24:35).

Luke now writes his last words for today. "Then he led them out as far as Bethany, and lifting up his hands he blessed them. While he blessed them, he parted from them, and was carried up into heaven. And they returned to Jerusalem with great joy, and were continually in the temple blessing God" (vs. 50-52).

Luke stretches and lays down his pen. He has finished his writing for today. He has led us from the amber room of soul death to the mountaintop where we blink back the sun's brightness and feel it warm our flesh.

Tomorrow he writes of the mighty acts of the Spirit done by

apostles touched by a risen Christ. He picks up the pen to jot down one last note for tomorrow's writing. "Day by day, attending the temple together and breaking bread in their homes, they partook of food with glad and generous hearts, praising God and having favor with all the people" (Acts 2:46, 47).

Ahead of us lie the mighty acts of the Spirit for us to do, for we too have known and sometimes been a touchable Jesus, we have been touched by a risen Christ.

Notes

1. Jonathan Edwards, *Treatise Concerning Religious Affections*, quoted in Don E. Saliers, *The Soul in Paraphrase*. The Seabury Press, 1980, p. 8.

2. John H. Westerhoff, III, *A Pilgrim People*. The Seabury Press, 1984, p. 4.

3. *Ibid.*

4. John Wesley, "May, 1738." *The Journal of the Reverend John Wesley, A.M.*, published in *The Works of John Wesley, Volume I*. London, England: Wesleyan Conference Office, 1872. Reprint edition, Salem, Ohio: Schmul Publishers, 1978, p. 103.

5. Michael Crosby, "Taking Brokenness into Ourselves," quoted in *Sharing one bread, sharing one mission*, ed. by Jean Stromberg. World Council of Churches, 1983, pp. 45-46.

6. Susanne K. Langer, *Philosophical Sketches*. Mentor, 1962, p. 141.

7. Lawrence Cada, S.M., *et al.*, *Shaping the Coming Age of Religious Life*. The Seabury Press, 1979, p. 89.

8. Peter M. Morgan, "Robert Richardson: Founder for Our Future." *Discipliana*, Vol. 44, No. 2 (Summer 1984), pp. 28-29.

9. Cloyd Goodnight and Dwight E. Stevenson, *Home to Bethphage*. Christian Board of Publication, 1949, pp. 83-84.

10. *Ibid.*, p. 141.

11. *Ibid.*, p. 164.

12. Urban T. Holmes, III, *Turning to Christ*. The Seabury Press, 1981, p. 2.

13. *Ibid.*, p. 5.

14. John E. Biersdorf, *Hunger for Experience*. The Seabury Press, 1975, pp. 135-136.

15. Howard Thurman, *The Growing Edge*. Harper & Brothers, 1956, pp. 176-178.

16. Wilhelm Pauck, quoted in Leonard I. Sweet, "The Four Fundamentalisms of Oldline Protestants." *The Christian Century*, Vol. 120, No. 9 (March 13, 1985), p. 270.

17. Parker J. Palmer, "Borne Again: The Monastic Way to Church Renewal." *The Auburn News*, Fall 1985, pp. 1-2.

18. *Ibid.*, pp. 5-6.

19. Mae Yoho Ward, *The Seeking Heart*, ed. by Don Ward. CBP Press, 1985, p. 82.

20. Guigo, II, *The Ladder of Monks*, tr. by Edmund Colledge, O.S.A. and James Walsh, S.J. Doubleday & Company, Inc., 1978, pp. 82-83.

21. *Ibid.*, (adapted) pp. 86-87.

22. Ronald Allen, "One-Shot Preaching." Seminar, 1985.

23. J. Cy Rowell, "The Future of Sunday Schools." *This is TCU*, Vol. 25, No. 3 (February 1983), p. 9.

24. Peter Ainslee quoted in W. W. Moore and E. Mack, *The New Standard Teacher Training Course*. Christian Board of Publication, 1918, p. 262.

25. Arlone Crowson, "A Worship Sharing." *Caring Ministry Newsletter*, Fall 1985, p. 4.

26. Martin E. Marty, "Mainline Churches: New Occasions Teach New Duties." *Action Information*, May-June 1985, p. 12.